THE REAL
MRS
BEETON

Other Books by Sheila Hardy

The Village School, Boydell Press/Anglia TV, 1979

1804 ... That was the Year ..., Brechinset, 1986

The Story of Anne Candler, SPA, 1988

The Diary of a Suffolk Farmer's Wife: 1854–69, Macmillan, 1992

Treason's Flame, Square One Publishing, 1995

Tattingstone: A Village and its People, self-published, 2000

The House on the Hill: the Samford House of Industry 1764–1930, self-published, 2001

Frances, Lady Nelson: the Life and Times of an Admirable Wife, Spellmount, 2005

The Cretingham Murder, The History Press, 2008

Arsenic in the Dumplings: A Casebook of Suffolk Poisonings, The History Press, 2010

THE REAL
MRS
BEETON

THE STORY OF
ELIZA
ACTON

BY SHEILA HARDY
FOREWORD BY DELIA SMITH

For Jasmine, Mina and Katie Hardy with my love

First published 2011

The History Press
The Mill, Brimscombe Port
Stroud, Gloucestershire, GL5 2QG
www.thehistorypress.co.uk

British Library Cataloguing in Publication Data.
A catalogue record for this book is available from the British Library.

ISBN 978 0 7524 6122 9

Typesetting and origination by The History Press
Printed in Great Britain

Contents

FOREWORD

BY DELIA SMITH

When I first received this manuscript I could hardly believe what was before me! Why? Let me begin by quoting my own words: 'Eliza Acton is the best cookery writer in the English language'. Her book *Modern Cookery for Private Families*, first published in 1845, has been a great inspiration – and had a great influence on me throughout my own years of cookery writing.

Yet, while I have studied her work very closely and often included her recipes in my own books, I have never had the least idea of who she was or where she came from. Though until now little has been known, Sheila Hardy has painstakingly researched and unravelled the mysterious background to this very accomplished and most significant cookery writer.

I personally am supremely grateful to have a much clearer understanding, and am pleased to have discovered a lot of what I had surmised to be affirmed. One thing I was convinced of was Eliza Acton never wrote a recipe she hadn't cooked herself. What I did not know was that her book took ten years to complete. She was a gifted writer and communicator, which is now explained by the fact that she started life as a poet and teacher.

I am also thrilled to discover some similarities between my heroine and myself. She quite definitely had a very similar mission: to help the inexperienced in a clear and simple way; in her own words 'which no other cookery book had yet done'. How I remember when I first started cooking –

great cooks, great cookbooks, but I was so often left wondering ... Eliza was actually the very first cookery writer to list precise amounts of ingredients at the end of her recipes.

In my early days the biggest puzzle for me was how on earth Mrs Beeton's book managed to utterly eclipse Eliza's far superior work. Now at last all is explained. I am deeply grateful to Sheila Hardy. This is an extremely important archive, not just for now but for anyone in future generations wishing to study the history of cooking in England.

PREFACE

I t is ironic in an age when fast-food outlets flourish and supermarkets vie
with each other to sell ready-prepared meals that can either be heated
in a microwave oven or boiled in plastic bags in a saucepan; and when
working women are said to have no time to cook a meal from scratch,
if indeed they even know how to, that designer kitchens should be a major
selling point in new houses and apartments and DIY chain stores sell
'dream kitchens' which once installed get very little use. What is even more
difficult to understand is the plethora of TV programmes which feature
cooking. Watching someone else cook has become a spectator sport. We sit
in comfort on our sofas to be entertained by amateurs giving dinner parties,
celebrity chefs showing how to create exotic dishes, or we are invited to
share the agony of contestants pitting their skills against each other in a
sort of X Factor for cooks. And when we are tired of watching, we can turn
to the books produced by the TV chefs to gaze in wonder at the colourful
illustrations and tantalise our taste buds as we read recipes, which we will
never attempt to make. Those who do cook will have a shelf of such books
but probably only one old favourite to which they continually refer. Cookery
books make up a large part of today's publishing market, but few of them
will have the success and longevity as the two major works of Eliza Acton.

Most modern cookery writers and chefs accept that they owe much to
the work done by Eliza Acton in the mid-years of the nineteenth century.
Indeed, there are some who claim that she still remains the *best* cookery

writer. Although her reputation was for a time eclipsed by Mrs Beeton, it is now acknowledged that that lady, during her short career, shamelessly plagiarised Acton's work while her publisher husband developed and manipulated his wife's name into a lucrative market brand. However, Acton's work continued to be published well into the twentieth century both in this country and abroad. And, again ironically, it has been the growing interest in celebrity chefs and cookery writers which has helped revive Eliza Acton's reputation and standing, leading to the publication in recent years of excellent reprints of her books.

Two features at least single her out from a long line of cookery writers. She was the first to produce a manual for general use in the home, one that encouraged the mistress of the house – and her daughters – as well as her cook, to understand the value of producing good, wholesome meals using fresh ingredients, cooked in the way best suited to them. Earlier male writers who worked as chefs in grand houses wrote books intended purely for wealthy households, where menus were lavish and cost unimportant and where there was a casual indifference to needless waste. But rarely, if ever, did any of these writers give specific instruction as to the exact quantities required for a dish or the length of time needed to prepare and then cook it. In her book, Acton followed the pattern of describing how the dish should be made, but then came her innovation. She was the first cookery writer, certainly in England, to add what we now take for granted: that all-important list of accurate measurements needed to produce a perfect result. She was indeed justified in calling her book *Modern Cookery in All its Branches* that later became known as *Modern Cookery for Private Families*, for she took into account the economic conditions which prevailed at the time; yet she also speaks clearly and soundly to the present age.

Eliza Acton was born in the last year of the eighteenth century, thus in many ways she belongs to the Georgian age. The decade preceding her birth had witnessed the French Revolution and England's wars against France, Holland and Spain; while her early years were dominated by the impact of the struggle against Napoleon. Indeed, it can be said that she lived through some of the momentous events in British modern history: Trafalgar and Waterloo; the abolition of the slave trade – the campaigner Thomas Clarkson and his wife who lived just outside Ipswich were subscribers to her early work; the imposition of the Corn Laws; the deaths of three kings and the accession of a young queen; the coming of the railways; the Great Exhibition; the Crimean War; and in the year of her death (1859) the publication of Darwin's *The Origin of Species*. What a source of historical information it would have been had she kept a diary of the daily happenings in her life, which also recorded events of national importance? We would have been able to read of the local celebratory ball held following the battle of Waterloo or the parties that were given for the marriage of the young Queen Victoria to her handsome consort Albert, as well as eyewitness accounts of starving rioters storming the flour mill just across the road from her home. Unfortunately, although she must have been a prolific letter writer and given the custom of the time she would have been unusual if she had not kept a diary, there is no archived store of letters or diaries.

So what is a biographer to do when it appears that her chosen subject has left nothing of a personal nature to posterity? Little has been written about Eliza Acton. A page or so is devoted to her on several sites on the Internet and she merits a mention in the *Dictionary of National Biography*. Thus we know when and where she was born and died, a brief note about her family and the fact that she started her writing career as a poet, having a volume of her poems published by subscription when she was 26. Although that book received good reviews and went into a second edition, later critics in the early twentieth century tended to dismiss her work as gloomy and sentimental. That she had talent as a writer is not in doubt; she also tried her hand at drama and had one of her plays produced in a London theatre. Given that this was the time when more and more women were able to earn a living writing novels for a market that was insatiable, it is surprising that Eliza Acton did not follow the same route as, for example, the Brontë sisters or Mrs Gaskell. So what turned her instead to writing about cookery? Legend has it that when she approached Thomas Longman to bring out a book of her new poems, the wily publisher, with a keen eye to the market and the great success his rival John Murray had enjoyed with Mrs Rundell's cookery book, told her to bring him a cookery book not poetry. If that is only half true, it already gives us a clue as to the character of the woman who was ready to take up the challenge rather than go away in a huff or take to her bed with a fit of the vapours. But it also shows that unlike some of those writers who followed her, she already possessed an interest in the subject.

In the absence of letters and diaries we are forced to look for much of our biographical information from Eliza's own written work. The poems are a great source for providing details of her relationships. From these we learn about her sisters and friends and, most importantly, about the great love affair that ended badly. And from her two books, *Modern Cookery* and *The English Bread Book*, we are able to pick up clues about her mature life, her wide circle of friends and acquaintances from all ranks of life. Every writer develops a 'voice' which should ring loud and strong throughout their work. It is when the reader can 'hear' the author talking to them, sharing ideas, offering opinions on all manner of subjects, that one knows that the book is successful. As one reads through the pages of *Modern Cookery*, one is not just being given a series of recipes, one is being made aware of Eliza's views on important topics of her day, ranging from the importance of education, both general and domestic, for women of all classes; the ghastly sweatshop conditions in commercial bakeries; the cramped living conditions of the poor; to the importance of growing one's own vegetables where possible. She was without doubt a campaigner, too, passionate about the poor nutrition of the nation as a whole; worried that the labourers and manual workers were insufficiently fed to do what was demanded of them, while richer men and women were destroying their health with an excess of food – but she is never strident. Gentle firmness is the line she adopts when standing at your elbow while you prepare a dish.

So, apart from Eliza's own work, where else can we seek information about her? The obvious place is in the newspapers, both those published nationally and those local to where she lived, and these have been drawn on heavily and have helped to clear up certain misinformation about her and her family which has appeared over the years. Also very useful are the genealogical sites which provide birth, marriage and death records, and the censuses from 1841 onwards. These, along with other documents, have been used with care to unravel her family background. Had Eliza taken to novel writing instead of cookery, she would have found sufficient in her own family history to write at least a three-volume family saga. Take a large family of mainly daughters, well educated and living in comfortable surroundings in a lively garrison town; throw into the plot some of the girls becoming governesses, a love affair or two, a short-lived marriage, tragic deaths, acts of bravery, time spent in France, a possible illegitimate child, a couple of doctors, the equivalent of a moonlight flit, a financial crisis that altered everyone's lives and there you would have had enough to keep Dickens going for weeks on end. It is said that Eliza met him – she certainly corresponded with him, but could she really have confided to him aspects of her family's history which are echoed in at least two of his novels?

The few facts known of Acton's life have been repeated so often that they have passed into mythology. One of these is that her father, John, was related to the ancient family of Suffolk Actons, of whom, during Eliza's childhood, the most direct descendant was Nathaniel Lee Acton of Bramford Hall. He was very active in the life of the town of Ipswich, attending social functions accompanied by his second wife, the former Penelope Rycroft, who like her predecessor had had her portrait painted by Romney. Our John Acton does not appear even in the remote branches of the Suffolk family tree, as we shall see later. The National Portrait Gallery has an etching by Spurgeon, taken from a portrait by Sir William Beechey, which has been copied on several occasions in publications and purports to be that of Eliza Acton. Quite how this mistake came about is hardly credible since the sketch plainly states that it is of *Mrs Acton* and it is dated *c*. 1803. Eliza was always referred to as 'Miss', but in any case, in 1803 she was only 4 years old. Neither is it likely that this was a portrait of her mother; it is almost certainly Mrs Nathaniel Lee Acton. Similar errors have been made about the number of sisters Eliza had and their marital status; how long Eliza spent in France and why; and other mysteries that will be unfolded later in what became almost a detective story.

For someone who was for some time a celebrity, why is it that none of her personal correspondence has survived? It would appear that of letters received by her, only four remain. It seems odd that she should have gone quite against the early nineteenth-century habit of keeping drafts of the letters she sent as well as those she received, especially as these were often copied to send on to others. Was it that in the years between 1840 to her death in 1859, she received so much from admiring readers that she hadn't room to store it all, or if the correspondent sent her a new recipe, she simply copied it to her files and destroyed the actual letter? But surely, she must have replied to those letters, so it seems strange that all these have been lost. Perhaps these words will stir someone, somewhere, to look again at that cache of old letters so carefully preserved by great-great-grandmamma.

On the other hand, it may be that Eliza, knowing the growing trend for biography, and having never hidden behind either a pen name or the usual soubriquet of 'a Lady' or 'a Gentlewoman' as others did, was anxious that her family history should remain within the family. It is possible that on her death bed she instructed her sister to destroy all her personal papers, thus keeping secret forever both the name of her faithless lover and if she really did give birth to a child out of wedlock.

Note: Nowadays, the word 'receipt' signifies the document which verifies payment for a purchase. Well into the first half of the nineteenth century, the word was still being used, as it long had, to describe the contents or make-up of either a dish in cooking or a prescription for a medicine. Since Eliza used it in her books, I have followed her example rather than substituting the more modern version 'recipe'. Certain items mentioned will also have changed, not least the decimalisation of both currency and weights. Eliza's original imperial weights have been retained throughout, but for anyone tempted to try her splendid receipts, it is worth noting that in her day, a pint was the equivalent to 16 fluid ounces rather than 20 as now. That might make the world of difference to your pudding!

Acknowledgements

Over the years I have been truly amazed by the tremendous kindness of complete strangers who have not only responded to my sometimes strange requests for information, but have gone out of their way to help. This time the response has been overwhelming. When I first dreamed up the idea of the biography of Eliza Acton I tentatively approached Elizabeth Ray, the food writer and editor of the Southover Editions of Eliza Acton's work, for her opinion. She not only gave her blessing but also most generously gave me her own notes and continued to answer my many questions. In the process I have gained a friend. Emboldened, and knowing of Delia Smith's declared admiration for Eliza Acton, I asked her, and she kindly agreed, to write the foreword. Jyll Bradley, the playwright, generously arranged with the BBC for me to have a recording of her play, *Before Beeton: the Eliza Acton Story*. In Sarah Death I discovered another Acton fan; the translator of Fredrika Bremer's work from the Swedish, she not only gave me free access to relevant articles, but also an introduction to an author who was unknown to me. Similarly, Dr Annie Gray went out of her way to share her enthusiasm for Eliza's cooking, as well as answering my questions. No longer able to travel to do my own research, I have had to rely on people like Nancy Fulford of Reading University, who scoured the ledgers and account books in the Longman Specials Collections for entries about Eliza. Mr & Mrs Anthony Wilson of the Tonbridge Historical Society kindly gave their expert knowledge, as did Beverley Matthews, senior librarian of Tonbridge School. My sincere and grateful thanks to them and also to the following for their help and encouragement: Pamela Henderson, Peggy Troll and Gill Squirrel studied some of the poems and gave their opinion of them. Glennis & Roger Pritchard and Mollie & Gordon Bolton combed the churchyards in Hastings and Grundisburgh for me. Dr E. Cockayne again helped with medical queries. Alan Best found useful material in the newspapers. Tony Copsey allowed me the use of illustrations from his collection, while Michael Riordan, Annabel Peacock and Andrew Lusted all made valuable contributions. The Ipswich branch of the Suffolk Record Office and the East Sussex Record Office at Lewes were most helpful, as was the British Library, Camden Borough Library and the Camden Registrars, and Ann Bagnall of The Southover Press. Special thanks too to The State Library of South Australia, The National Library of Australia and the University of California Davis, all of whom offered not only prompt help and kindness but furthered my amazement at the wonders of email and the Internet. On a very personal note, I could not have completed this work without the assistance of my three 'special research assistants' – Patricia Burnham, as always, was in at the beginning and undertook a great deal of the genealogical research; Fiona Scorer took care of the research in London and much else, and then, just when I most needed help, a chance meeting with Rachel Field led to her offering to undertake additional local research, and, as it turned out, much more beside. To each and every one of you, including probably the most important, Sophie Bradshaw, who took the risk that Eliza Acton's story should reach the public, please accept my deepest gratitude.

ONE

BEGINNINGS

Right from the outset, Eliza Acton stood out from the rest her family. Unlike her six sisters and three brothers, she was born not in the East Anglian port of Ipswich but in Battle, near the historically famous south coast town of Hastings. It was there on 5 June 1799 that she was baptised in the parish church within a year of the marriage of her parents, John and Elizabeth, *née* Mercer, which had taken place in the bride's home parish of East Farleigh in Kent. It has long been supposed that John was in some way related to the old established Suffolk Acton family, mainly because that might account for how he came to be working in Ipswich. And the fact that Eliza was born in Sussex rather than Suffolk has been glossed over by suggesting that John had been visiting there in order to sort out the financial affairs of an uncle, believed to be the town clerk of Hastings.

However, that was not the case at all. John himself was born in Hastings in 1775, one of the seven children of Joseph Acton and Elizabeth *née* Slatter of Tonbridge in Kent. Elizabeth's mother owned property in Battle where several of her late husband's family still lived, which may explain how Joseph came to meet her. Both Eliza's grandmothers were linked with these towns in Kent, which were later to feature in Eliza's life. But perhaps more importantly they both probably had some money in their own right. And it was not his uncle, but John's father Joseph who, among other things, was the town clerk of Hastings. There is no baptismal record for Joseph Acton in East Sussex so his early years are still shrouded in mystery, and it was not until 1762 that he first appears in any official record of the town. He had by then completed his training to be an attorney at law, so he was probably around 21 years old. In order to make a living that would enable him eventually to marry and have a family, he would have needed more than the fees gained from drawing up wills, conveyancing property and sorting out legal problems for individual clients. The solution to this was to take on some form of paid office under the Crown. In order to do that, he had to swear both the oath of allegiance to the Crown and also prove that he was a communicant member of the Church of England. At this period both Catholics and Dissenters were unable 'to bear any office, receive pay or hold office from the Crown'. So those aspiring to such positions were expected to present themselves at their parish church and 'receive the sacrament of the Lord's Supper according to the usage of the Church of England'. The actual wording of the document refers to the specific denial of the belief in the transubstantiation of the bread and wine used in the service, which was intended to flush out any covert Roman Catholic. In order to receive the all-important Sacramental Certificate, the officiating minister and his churchwarden had to sign that they had witnessed the applicant actually receiving the bread and wine, and just to make doubly sure that all was in order, two independent witnesses from the congregation were required to make an affirmation. Many of those listed as being in receipt of Sacramental Certificates were excise officers, customs officers and local mayors, but when Joseph, described as 'of Battle', made his profession of faith in Westham church on 1 October 1762, he was about to become town clerk of Pevensey.

The following year when he again made the declaration he was described as Joseph Acton, gent, a prized appellation that was to remain in all future records. By 1768 he was the acting coroner for Rye, having the previous year become the deputy steward of the Manor of Wilmington, a position he held until 1786. To these he added the position of town clerk of Hastings in 1767, by which time he had settled in that town and his eldest son Walter was the first of his seven children to be baptised in All Saints church in December of that year. Joseph continued as town clerk until 1781. In addition to acting as solicitor to several private families in the area, he was also made steward of the Manor of Mayfield in 1772.

All Saints church, Hastings. (Courtesy of Glennis & Roger Pritchard)

A very busy man, it would appear he was both respected – he had been made a Freeman – and had made a good living. In time, his eldest son Walter would follow his father's profession in the law and young John was being educated to join him.

It would seem, however, that Joseph was not as skilful in his personal financial dealings as he should have been, and when he died in 1788 there was a shock in store for the family. Having had much experience in drawing up wills for others, his own was a fine example of business-like brevity. Unexpectedly, he starts his bequests by leaving to his wife not his estate, but all the wood, coal, liquors and provisions that were in his house at the time of his death. He then gets straight to the point: he is in debt, having borrowed from various sources unspecified sums which he knows he is unable to repay. Honourably, he wishes all these debts to be repaid in full and the only way

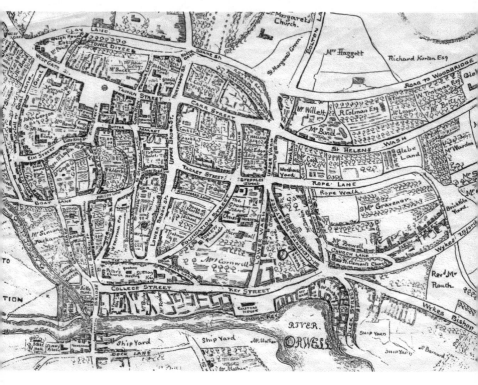

Map of Ipswich, 1778

this can be done is by selling everything he possesses: 'all and every my messuages [houses with land attached and outbuildings], buildings, lands, tenements and hereditaments [inherited property] as well as all my goods, chattels, rights, credits and all my real and personal estate whatsoever and wheresoever'. He appointed four gentlemen friends as trustees, requesting that they sell for the best possible price the whole lot or as much of it as would be necessary to repay all debts, funeral expenses and legal fees. Whatever was left was to go to his widow, but in the event that she should die before settlement had been made – and as a lawyer Joseph was fully aware of how long settlement could take – then the residue was to be shared equally among his children. The trustees were also appointed guardians of any child under the age of 21, which was all four of those living, although Walter had almost reached his majority.

On the few facts available to us, it would seem that the widow and her family were to be left homeless and destitute, but it is doubtful that this was the case, even if they had to move from the family home to somewhere smaller. Elizabeth did have some money of her own, as well as relations with businesses in Battle, and they no doubt would have offered assistance. Had 13-year-old John not been destined for the law as his father intended, he might well have found himself apprenticed to his uncle George Slatter, learning the diverse business of grocer, cheesemonger, dealer in china and seller of wines and spirits. That, however, might have been preferable to working for his aunt, Mrs John Slatter, who was a butcher. Instead, in the years that followed, John armed himself with the skills that would find him employment in business: knowledge of the law, accountancy and the ability to read and write documents. It is possible that he joined his brother Walter as a solicitor before embarking on an early marriage, but there are hints that he and Walter had a disagreement, which left John seeking to move away from Hastings.[1] Perhaps, it was through his uncle George's connection with the wine trade that John eventually secured the position with Trotman, Halliday & Studd of Ipswich and thus began his career of handling the business side of running a brewery. However it came about, by 1800 Mr and Mrs Acton and the baby Eliza had left Sussex and taken up residence in the house that adjoined St Peter's Brewery in Dock Street, Ipswich.

Ipswich was very different to the small town of Hastings. Situated at the meeting of the River Gipping with the tidal estuary of the Orwell, the town had a history stretching back to prehistoric times. On the flat land around the two rivers settlement had grown up, sheltered by hills which provided plentiful freshwater springs. Today, the almost circular central shopping area still follows the street patterns laid down in early medieval times. If John Acton came back today, he would still be able to find his way from Dock Street, over Stoke Bridge, past St Peter's church and up to the Cornhill at the centre of the town. The town's prosperity had always lain with its port activity. In the years when East Anglia was the centre of the woollen trade, most of its produce was exported through Ipswich. Shipyards lined the banks of the Orwell building both commercial and naval vessels. Trade flourished with other parts of the country, fresh meat, dairy products and meat, for example, being carried regularly to feed London's population. Ipswich ships carried coal from Newcastle around the coast, while other vessels ventured up to Greenland to fish for whales to satisfy the eighteenth-century demand for lighting oil. The import and export trade carried by foreign ships meant that Ipswich inhabitants were quite accustomed to hearing foreign voices in their shops and inns. The town, too, became home to exiles from the Continent, Flemish weavers, Huguenot silk workers from France, Jews from Holland – all had something to contribute to the life of the town and all tended to settle in the already overcrowded parish of St Clement on the town side of the docks.

When the Actons arrived, the town was experiencing a further increase in its population, this time from a great influx of the military for the town had long been a garrison for holding troops waiting to be shipped to fight against England's enemies on the Continent. And there had been several of these during the latter part of the eighteenth century. Housing troops temporarily had always been a problem, but now it had been realised that requisitioning inns and taverns and empty commercial buildings, as well as large private houses, was, for many reasons, not the best way to solve it. So the decision had been taken to erect a permanent purpose-built barracks on land to the west of the town in the parish of St Matthews. The building, completed in 1795, was soon in use and would continue to be so once the war against France was announced. When Nelson's wife, Fanny,[2] was waiting in Bath prior to moving into their newly acquired home on the outskirts of Ipswich in 1798, she was perturbed to receive news that requisitioning was in operation again in the town. She wrote to beg that her correspondent should place a bed in the house (indicating its occupancy) and to let it be known that she was coming very shortly. But even the new barracks was not sufficient to house the number of troops who would occupy the town over the next twenty years and Eliza would have grown up with soldiers almost next door in a commandeered Maltings building.

It was not only the military – and their hangers-on – who had swelled the town's population. Many who had suddenly found that living in London was becoming too expensive, moved their households to Ipswich where the rents were lower and the cost of living much less. These incomers added to the town's already growing middle class, as well as the county gentry from the surrounding countryside who looked to Ipswich to provide them with social activities. The annual race week which was held in July was perhaps the highlight of the social calendar, but throughout the summer there were many opportunities for gatherings: balls, breakfast parties (held late morning), fête champêtres, concerts in the Assembly Rooms and stage plays at the newly built theatre in Tankard Street. Those like the prosperous brewer John Cobbold, who lived with his second wife Elizabeth at his estate called Holywells, frequently entertained guests both within their home and at outdoor parties in the extensive grounds overlooking the Orwell. Mrs Cobbold, herself a multi-talented woman, did much to encourage the artistic life of the town. She regularly gave concerts to showcase local talent, encouraging young singers and musicians, or providing budding poets and playwrights with an opportunity to present their work to an audience. It was she who encouraged both the young artists Gainsborough and Constable. Her influence on the cultural life of the town was far-reaching, ill deserving Charles Dickens' cruel satire of her in *The Pickwick Papers*.[3]

But while those with money and free time sought amusement, there were other incomers to the town. The decline in agricultural jobs and the demand for labour in the developing industries within the town had

Stoke Street, close to the Acton home, 1886. (Sketch by Elizabeth Cotton, from the collection of A. Copsey)

'Bloomfield's Buildings, 1887, at the back of Stoke Street'. Courtyard housing off Stoke Street. (Sketch by Elizabeth Cotton, from the collection of A. Copsey)

brought an influx of the labouring classes seeking employment. That there was insufficient work to go round soon became apparent and a huge strain was placed on the individual town parishes, which were responsible for providing Poor Relief. If the Actons had arrived at the beginning of January 1800, they must have been appalled by the numbers of starving people seen in the streets. Robert Trotman, John Acton's new employer, an elected bailiff of the town on several occasions, had just been made treasurer for the Public Fund for Relieving the Distress of the Poor. As money and donations in kind poured in, the immediate need was to provide warm sustenance in the form of soup. So dire was the situation that *The Ipswich Journal* devoted almost a whole page to the ingredients that went into the soup. Meat, preferably on the bone, was stewed until the bones were clean, at which point they would be split to extract the marrow from them. Potatoes, white cabbage, peas – coarse field peas that were the basis of pease pudding – barley and onions were added to the mixture. That the directions for the making of the soup were so detailed suggests that the recipe was included for other towns and villages in the area to copy, and even that it was intended for a more personal use. Certainly in her later years, Eliza Acton would have appreciated the care that was taken in the preparation of the soup and the understanding that good nourishment was vitally important for health.

John and Elizabeth settled into their new home on the Stoke side of the river. Less crowded than the other side, their commodious house had the advantage of the fresh air from the open country with the hills beyond. Sadly, their next child, a boy called John like his father, did not survive long, but he was soon followed in 1801 by a healthy girl, named Anna after one of John's sisters, and at the end of December 1802 Catherine arrived to join her sisters in the nursery. Fortunately, neither Eliza nor Anna would have been aware of the turmoil within the country as a whole, when in the summer of 1803 it appeared that the threat of invasion was imminent. It was almost the sole topic of conversation at the three-day race meeting at the beginning of July, where the numbers of the great and the good of Town and County had been swollen by the large number of officers from the military. In the coffee houses in town and over the teacups in private houses news was exchanged of the letters from friends and colleagues living in France, which brought constant proof that the French government was determined to invade. The London newspaper reports corroborated this by relating that the enemy's Minister of the Interior had sent a circular letter to every town and department in France giving orders for the construction of flat-bottomed boats capable of transporting troops across the Channel. It was believed that use would also be made of the shallow-draught Dutch schuyts, which were capable of running right on shore depositing a hundred men at a time on the beaches.

The British government tried to play down all the rumours, reassuring the nation that such an event was highly unlikely, the French Army being totally unprepared to face the large and well-disciplined British Army they would find awaiting them. But the populace was not so sure. Reliable reports from Brussels brought news of very active invasion preparations. It was said that once the harvest was gathered in, 200,000 men would be mobilised. The figures quoted were impressive: 80,000 men were ready in Cherbourg; Compiègne and St Omer would each muster 50,000, and another 40,000 would come from Batavia. Flotillas of gunboats were to be assembled at Dunkirk, Boulogne and Calais, and – it was said – Napoleon himself would command the attack. To counter this, His Majesty King George III declared that he personally would lead his troops into battle.

However, his history of illness over recent years did little to reassure his subjects, even though the press accompanied this announcement with a reminder to readers of the inspirational speech Queen Elizabeth had made at Tilbury some 200 years earlier while awaiting the attack of the Spanish Armada. She might have been but a 'weak and feeble woman', but she not only possessed the strong stomach of a man, she was also in full command of her mental faculties.

Just how serious the situation had become was made apparent to John Acton when, on 5 August 1803, he was obliged to submit a rough estimate of his firm's stock-in-trade as part of the government's evacuation plans. As manager of the firm Trotman, Halliday & Studd, such business was left to him. Trotman was far too busy with all his civic affairs, and membership of sundry committees took up much of his time. The other partners also had their own interests, the brewery merely an investment for the capital they had to spare. Edward Studd was a retired seafarer who had for many years captained a vessel belonging to the East India Company. The reward for his long service had brought him a small fortune, some of which was invested in the brewery. Although not personally involved in the routine business of the firm, the captain would have taken a keen interest in the seaworthiness of the ships which carried the cargoes they sold, particularly if the firm held shares in any of those vessels, as was frequently the case. Simon Halliday, on the other hand, a Scot who came from a wealthy family settled in Dumfries, brought other expertise. He had trained for a career in medicine and had for a time sailed on the West Indies Station as a naval surgeon, which is probably how he came to marry the daughter of a wealthy plantation owner in Jamaica. Thereafter, he gave up both the sea and medicine to become a banker, a career that seems to have evolved from his lending out money in the form of mortgages to cash-starved gentlemen in Jamaica, where, for example, after supplying a number of mortgages on the Castle Wemyss sugar estate, he eventually had the whole estate conveyed to him when the owner was unable to meet his commitments. Halliday would have known about the import/export business not only of sugar but also of rum, an outlet for which he had through the brewery. Young John Acton must have been in awe of all three partners, but Halliday was obviously the most prestigious, being a respected authority in various fields. In 1801 his medical knowledge led to his appointment as a member of the Board of Health to the Government in Bombay, while in 1825 he became a director – and possibly major shareholder – of the Australian Agricultural Company. Who knows why he chose to invest in the St Peter's Brewery, but his involvement with the town was not simply one of business. In spite of having a house in Lower Berkeley Square in London, and a property known as Whinnyrig on the banks of the Solway Firth, Halliday had a home in Ipswich, too. In fact, when his wife died in 1817 at their London home, her obituary described her as wife of Simon Halliday Esq. of Ipswich.

Complying with the government order, John Acton made his list, now preserved in the Suffolk Record Office, on a small scrap of paper, for paper had become both expensive and hard to get. The official instructions had required 'a rough estimate', so he wrote that there were at that time 63 vats of various sizes holding about 95,940 gallons of beer. Then there were about 7,351 gallons of old beer and porter – the really strong stuff – as well as Brown SP and common ale. As for the ingredients needed for his trade, he had 4,500 bushels of malt, 1,600 bushels of barley and 200 of wheat. He also had a stock of beans and peas, 120 bushels of the former and 80 of the latter. There was 12,600 hundredweight of coal and 800 barrels and casks. Finally, he wrote that there was a cart and two draft horses which would be available to provide transport for those who needed it. Appending the words 'signed for Robert Trotman, Esq.' he added his own clear signature, John Acton.

The paper was duly sent to the overseers, the two elected representatives of St Peter's Parish, who, like their counterparts throughout the country, were charged with collecting and collating the information ready for the mass evacuation should it become necessary. Should the word come, transmitted by the semaphore system installed in the towers of churches in line from the coast, or by beacon should it be night, that the French were closing in, those living within 15 miles of the coast would be the first to move. This would, of course, include the inhabitants of Ipswich. Inland destinations had been designated to receive them, but the populace was advised to follow routes that would not impede troop movements. In order that no one should be left behind, it was essential for the authorities to know just what transport was available for those who did not possess their own – hence John's placing the brewery cart and horses at the parish's disposal. It was also essential to be able to feed the evacuees, thus a tally was made of cattle and all other forms of livestock and perhaps, more important, finding intelligent and active people who could undertake the removal of all animals. Horses not required to draw vehicles were to be removed first as they were considered of most use to the enemy. The local inventory also collected the names of millers and bakers, as well as the number of barges and boats which could be pressed into service. Once the enemy had landed, every man who possessed firearms or swords would band together in groups of between twenty-five and thirty-five to form a volunteer force or Home Guard. Those mounted were to be known as the Volunteer Yeomanry; those on foot the Volunteer Infantry. Each group was to elect its own leader, though one suspects that in many cases this was a foregone conclusion rather than a democratic election. Those who were not armed were just as useful in their own way and they were to form companies of Pioneers, armed with pickaxes and other tools such as pitchforks, spades, shovels, billhooks and saws. Grouped in twenty-fives, the Pioneers when on service would be paid the standard day rate for an agricultural worker. The group leader would receive 3s a day, while the captain who had overall responsibility for groups of fifty received 5s daily.

Already those known as out-Chelsea Pensioners, former military men living in the community, had received notice to report for possible recall to their regiments. Only those over 60 who had lost a limb, been blinded or crippled or were in possession of a certificate of total unfitness were exempt from the call-up. And in the docks and villages either side of the river, the Press Gangs were out in full force to find men for service on board warships. Magistrates passing sentence on criminals now offered service in the Navy as an alternative to a term in gaol. No man was safe from service of some sort except Moravians or Quakers, who were exempt by their religious faith.[4]

However, some must have actively enjoyed this period of heightened activity with its mixture of fear and excitement. One such was John's director, Edward Studd. On the day after John had filed his report of the firm's assets, Captain Studd, along with 130 seamen, congregated in the yard of the grammar school in nearby Foundation Street to volunteer to Captain Edge of the Royal Navy his service in the Sea Fencibles. This, the naval equivalent of the military volunteer force, had been formed in 1798 but disbanded during the peace of Amiens. The fishermen, boatmen, bargees and so on who volunteered did so with alacrity since it made them immune from the predatory Press Gang. As for officers to command them, there was no shortage of ageing naval men who were on half pay. Studd had probably been one of the leaders of the initial formation and no doubt relished the opportunity to put his expertise to good use. In smaller gunboats than those used by the Navy, he and his men would take to the sea to form part of the blockade off the British coast to deter the invaders.

A week later, news came that communication with France via Calais was at an end. All mail to France now had to be dispatched twice a week via Gothenburg in Sweden. It was also announced that the government was considering registering all the aliens in Britain. Bearing in mind that many French aristocrats had sought refuge in Britain, either just before or immediately after the Revolution in France, this was no easy task, particularly as many had brought their household staff with them, some of whom had since dispersed throughout the country and taken new employment with English families. In some areas fears grew that any foreigner might be a spy for Napoleon. But by the beginning of September, legislation was in place that all foreigners who were French, or subjects of a country under French rule or at war with Great Britain, who had arrived after 1 October 1801, were to leave the country. This gave dispensation to those émigrés who had sought refuge at the time of the Revolution. Those in London were given less than fifteen days to depart, the rest were to go before 20 September. Exemption was granted to foreign ambassadors and their servants, those who had received special licences, and – much to the relief of wealthy English citizens – those they employed as domestic servants, especially if they had arrived in the country before the October 1801 deadline.

While there was tremendous military activity in the Ipswich area, with the Duke of York coming to review the garrison and the Ipswich Volunteers, as well as the regiments encamped outside the town on Rushmere Heath, life went on almost unaltered for the upper classes. Those who normally took a late summer holiday in Aldeborough continued to do so, including Robert Trotman and his family. And for tradespeople and entrepreneurs the war was providing new opportunities. One such was a Mr Masters, a tailor by trade, who offered his services as a supplier of uniforms for the Volunteer regiments throughout the county. His advertisement gives us a clear indication of what was worn, namely a jacket, pantaloons and half gaiters, a black stock, round hat and feather. The complete uniform, at a cost to each member of the corps of £1 18s 6d, was available for inspection at his house in Ipswich. To counteract any suggestion of profiteering, he assured the public that the pattern and the price had been approved by the Lord Lieutenant of the county. Recognising individual taste, Mr Masters offered breeches and long gaiters as an alternative to pantaloons at no extra cost.

Trotman, Studd & Halliday no doubt also benefited from the demand for their products. With so many soldiers in town the supplies of the beer houses would have needed continuous replenishment, while the officers would be demanding supplies of wine and spirits. All in all it was a strange time. On the one hand there was great fear for what the future held, on the other the present was a time of prosperity for some. The question was how long would it last and what would be its effects?

TWO

THE FAMILY

B y the time peace was finally restored twelve years later in 1815, John and Elizabeth Acton's family had increased to nine. Following Eliza, Anna and Catherine there was a two-year gap before the arrival of the first surviving son, Edward, in 1805. He was followed by four more daughters: Mary Mercer (1808), Susannah Edgar (1810), Helen (1811) and Lucy (1812). Two further sons, Edgar (1813) and John Theobald Studd (1815) completed the family. Before the reader realises there is a mistake in the number given, it is necessary to relate a sad incident. On Monday 24 June 1812, the coroner and a panel of jurors assembled at the Actons' house in Dock Street for the inquest into the sudden death of baby Lucy. Maria Simpson, the child's nursemaid, was called before them to explain the circumstances of the infant's death. She explained that on the Monday before, Lucy had been what she called 'rather troublesome'. No specific cause was mentioned, but given that the baby was only a few weeks old it was likely to have been colic, which causes great distress to a child and is accompanied by prolonged bouts of crying. Maria had resorted to laudanum drops, the remedy of the period in an attempt to give both of them some relief.[5] She had given Lucy about a quarter of a teaspoonful. This, alas, had more than quietened the child; it killed her. The distraught Maria obviously feared for her own life but the jury brought in a sympathy verdict of misadventure, exonerating her on the grounds that she had not had 'any malicious or bad intention rather the contrary'.

An unexplained result of this death was that the baby was not buried in St Peter's graveyard but interred instead in that of St Mary Stoke, just across the road from Dock Street and in a different parish.

It may seem odd that four of the children bear surnames as first, second or third baptismal names. This was a usual practice of the time and gives us a clue about who the Actons were particularly friendly with or who they wished to flatter by giving that person's name to their child. Mary bore her mother's maiden name as her second name. Often it was the first child of the marriage who was named for the maternal family, so it is somewhat strange that John and Elizabeth waited until Mary's birth to acknowledge the Kentish side of the family. Possibly Mrs Acton, seeing that her brother John was set on a steady career as a banker, decided he was a sensible choice to cultivate. Susannah, on the other hand, was given the name of one of the leading families in Suffolk. Different branches of the Edgar family lived at The Red House in Ipswich or in the adjoining village of Westerfield. Milesom Edgar, in particular, was at the forefront of much of the decision-making within the town. One of his many charitable offices was as chairman of the local Humane Society, which was active in deciding to whom medals should be awarded for acts of bravery. It was from him that young Edgar Acton acquired his first name, and years later Eliza was to pay her own tribute to the culinary delights found at the Edgars' dining table. Poor baby John, a delicate child, had to bear the names not only of his father but also of two important local men. John Medows Theobald, Esquire, lived at Claydon Hall, just outside Ipswich. Descended from an old established Suffolk family, he served as high sheriff of the county in 1787, was a long-serving magistrate as well as a major in the Yeomanry, and was well respected by all with whom he came into contact. When he died at the age of 81 in 1830, his obituary noted that 'for hospitality and liberality he could be equalled but not surpassed'. Quite what his connection was with the Acton family is not known, but John and Elizabeth must have had a very good reason for adopting his name for their child.

Edward Studd, who provided John's third name, played a major part in the Actons' business life. When Robert Trotman died, Studd had become the major shareholder in the business, which consisted of the brewery, the Maltings, various inns, shops and residential property both in Ipswich and Harwich. John was offered the opportunity to become a junior partner

Corner of the Cornhill and Tavern Street, Ipswich (1794–1812). (From a drawing by
George Frost)

in the business, but it is likely that he had to borrow heavily to do so. The new partnership of Studd, Halliday & Acton announced itself in *The Ipswich Journal* of 30 March 1811, describing themselves as brewers, wine, brandy, coal and corn merchants, as well as providers of fine ale, brown stout, porter and table beer for private families. Their wine, spirits, malt and corn, they claimed, were of the best quality. The business was now in a position to expand and in October 1813 they announced in the press that they had taken over the stock-in-trade of the old established business of a Mrs King. Studd himself died that year, leaving his share of the business to his wife, so no doubt the naming of the baby could be considered as both a tribute to her late husband and a compliment to her. That left Simon Halliday as the strongest financial force in the business. The fact that none of the Acton children were given his name suggests that relations between Halliday and John were kept on a purely business basis.

Twenty-first-century family historians always marvel at the size of families in earlier periods of history, wondering how they were all accommodated, often within very small houses. The quick answer is that apart from when the first few children were very small, in most cases it was unlikely that the whole family was ever together for any length of time. In middle and upper class families new babies were often put out to wet nurses, who might live at some distance if it was a case of a town child being sent to the country. Here the child might stay for a couple of years, before returning to its parental home for several years, before being sent away again, this time to school. If the family was growing rapidly and income was limited, then one or even more children from the family might be adopted by a wealthy or perhaps childless relation. Delicate children could find themselves living with elderly grandparents rather than having to face the hurly-burly of family life; while the future captains of the British Navy were sent to sea as midshipmen as young as 12, the same age as the labourers' children were considered old enough to start work. Whether they were entering one of the many branches of domestic service, agricultural labour, or apprenticeship to a trade, then living accommodation was usually provided as part of their terms of employment. Thus space at home was made for those growing up behind them.

Space was not necessarily a problem for the Actons, the house in Dock Street being of generous proportions. A sale of some, if not all, of their household furniture in 1827 revealed that they had at least five four-poster or tent beds. This may not sound adequate for a family of eleven, but if we put two to a bed and place the youngest in cots, then the entire family could have been comfortably accommodated. We know from our reading of novels of the period that siblings, especially females, in middle-class families shared beds as a matter of course, often until they finally left the family home. The Acton home was furnished, as one would expect of a prosperous man of business. There were Brussels carpets in the main reception rooms and rugs on the floor of the bedchambers. All the chests of drawers, wardrobes, washstands, chairs and tables were of solid mahogany. They possessed more than one dining table, suggesting that they had a morning or breakfast room as well as the more formal dining room with its matching table and chairs – a set of twelve chairs being the norm. The drawing room had at least two sofas with their accompanying sofa tables, more chairs and a pair of inlaid card tables, which show one of the ways Mr and Mrs Acton entertained guests in the evening. Paintings and what were described as 'valuable prints' hung on the walls of the principal rooms. All this suggests either inherited goods or affluence. But what marked the Acton household out as belonging to a cultured family, as well as a reasonably affluent one given the price of books, was the fact that a library of 400 books was included in the auction sale. How many families today can equal that?

It seems likely that the children would have received their earliest education at home. However, when it came to more formal schooling, Ipswich was generously supplied with schools and academies for both young ladies and young gentlemen. We have to bear in mind that the term 'school' conveyed a very different picture in the eighteenth and nineteenth century to the one that replaced it after 1870, when elementary education became compulsory and so introduced vast buildings to house pupils. These buildings grew to a size which earlier generations would have found hard to comprehend. Even the old established grammar schools and public schools rarely had as many as 100 pupils. Freed from any government control or interest, most schools in the Actons' day were small affairs run, in the main, in private houses. Clergymen supplemented their stipends by taking five or six young men into their vicarages and giving them a solid Classical education that would lead to their perhaps going on to a public or grammar school for two or three years prior to going to university. In towns, small establishments, both day and boarding, prepared boys for a career in business or the services by specialising in mathematics and the sciences. While the old established grammar and endowed schools, which had been founded long before to provide a free education for poor bright boys, still functioned in premises that had changed little since Elizabethan times, now their endowment was insufficient and they had to rely on fee-paying scholars to keep them going. As with all things, some educational establishments were of very poor quality, some being little more than places in which children were 'dumped' for a small fee and forgotten. Charles Dickens and Charlotte Brontë highlighted the worst examples, Lowood[6] being a very different place to the gentle/genteel establishment run by Mrs Goddard in Jane Austen's *Emma*.

Often it was the educated widow and her unmarried daughters who needed to add to a small income in order to keep a roof over their heads, who used their talents to pass on their own knowledge to young ladies. In return for quite a moderate fee they would instruct their young charges in the basics of reading, writing and arithmetic. As they grew older they would expand their reading to include Classical authors and poets, and they would be encouraged to produce what we now call 'creative writing'. And all these essays and verses were to be executed with the most careful penmanship. The 'Italian hand' was fashionable at the time and Mr Harmer, who had a boarding school in Ipswich, made a little extra income by acting as an agent for pens which he sold at between 4s and 14s per 100. The fine pens specially adapted for use in executing the Italian hand were no doubt at the top end of the price range. So no slovenly handwriting for Miss, who was also taught different branches of mathematics, mainly arithmetic and the keeping of accounts. History, geography and botany also featured on the syllabus, as did needlework and general art lessons. However, if a girl showed a particular leaning towards art, then she might well take extra lessons from a visiting tutor. Similarly, basic instruction in French, music and dancing could be supplemented by weekly visits from peripatetic masters. The quality of the teaching given depended greatly on the expertise of the schoolmistresses, but it was probably a great deal better than we have been led to believe – witness the number of women writers who emerged in the nineteenth century displaying a breadth and depth of knowledge that perhaps is lacking today.

This knowledge was not confined to the Arts as we might suppose, for many middle-class girls were given the opportunity to study mathematics and the sciences in depth. Those fortunate enough to have fathers who encouraged their daughters to study, or gave them the opportunity to learn with their brothers if they were being tutored at home, often went on to become experts in such subjects as astronomy or, as in the case of Suffolk-born Laetitia Jermyn (1788–1848), Lepidoptera. Her book *The Butterfly Collector's Vade Mecum* was published in 1822. Admittedly, her stepfather, Ipswich printer John Raw, was the publisher but Miss Jermyn, who also wrote poetry and biographies, was recognised as an authority in her field. Although she was twelve years Eliza Acton's senior, it is possible that they knew each other and Jermyn might well have been a role model for the young Eliza. Another expert in her field, Mrs Jane Loudon (1807–58), wrote prolifically, passing on her knowledge and expertise of gardening in books such as *Plain Instructions in Gardening; The Villa Gardener: Comprising the Choice of a Suburban Villa Residence; The Laying Out, Planning and Culture of the Garden and Grounds etc; and The Year-Book of Natural History, for Young Persons*. Much of the material contained in these books she used in her weekly magazine, *The Ladies' Companion at Home and Abroad*. Started in 1849, the content of this magazine and others that followed it show the great interest there was among middle-class women – and working-class ones, too, for the literate female servants who worked in households where the mistress subscribed to the magazine often had the opportunity to read and learn from it. *The Ladies' Companion* was later to provide an outlet for Eliza Acton's articles on *Household Hints and Receipts*.

But that was in the future. First Eliza had to complete her own education. John Acton had never let go the belief that he came from a 'good family' and that his children should be brought up in a manner that fitted that status. That he also believed in the importance of education for its own sake is without doubt, hence the large number of books in the home which the children were encouraged to read, but he must have been realistic enough to consider that although his family mixed socially with some of the leading figures in the town, it might be difficult to find husbands for all six of his daughters. Since he would find it hard to support the unmarried ones for life, it was important that they should be equipped to make their own way in the world if necessary. Thus they would have had the best education available to prepare them either to take their place in society as wives of gentlemen, or as schoolmistresses or governesses, the latter occupation, of course, sometimes leading to marriage to an employer.

It is not known if the girls were day pupils in the town itself or if they were sent as boarders to some other town in Suffolk. If they were to have the advantage of specialist masters in music, art and French, then it would seem most sensible for them to have attended a school in the town where all these things were readily available. In addition, they would have been able to attend performances at the theatre and concerts in the Assembly Rooms or at one of the town churches. Ipswich boasts some very fine medieval churches, too many now to support the dwindling number of churchgoers actually living in the town itself. Fortunately, several of these lovely old buildings have been given a new lease of life. At St Peter's nowadays, while listening to a concert given by the Ipswich Town Band who have their headquarters there, it is possible to sit and gaze at the beautiful Tournai marble font where most of the Acton children were baptised. Two hundred years ago the Acton family might well have attended concerts there, too, given by one or other of the regimental bands stationed in the town.

John Acton was steadily becoming well known, not just in the brewing industry but also as a reputable person often assigned to collect the debts due to other businessmen, including those who were deceased. This suggests that he was operating in a legal capacity and it is possible that he is the John Acton who was granted a B. Law from St John's College, Cambridge, in 1812. An advertisement in November 1811 gently requests 'debtors to pay accounts to Mr J Acton on behalf of John Smith', who had been a cooper at the brewery. However, by 1813 the tone of a press notice was decidedly more aggressive: 'Those who stand indebted to Thomas Selby of Ipswich Upholsterer, are requested to pay the amount of the debt to Mr J Acton of Ipswich beer brewer and Mr Richard Frankland, linen draper, his assignees, by 20 February, otherwise compulsory methods will be used for the recovery thereof.'

From 1813–17 John also played a major role in the parochial life of St Peter's. It is important to remember that in those days that meant a great deal more than that which revolved round the spiritual life of the church. The parish, that is all the houses and businesses within its boundaries, represented the lowest band of English government, being responsible for the collection of the local Poor Rate[7] payable on each property and then using it wisely for the care of needy members within the parish, the widows and orphans, the sick and impaired, as well as the unemployed. At the Annual Parish Meeting, which was open to all the ratepayers, four officials were elected from within their number to hold office for the year – two churchwardens and two overseers. John was elected an overseer for the first time in 1813. This was a trusted and time-consuming position, since it was up to the overseers both to set and collect the Poor Rate for the parish and then administer the funds, deciding who was entitled to what. One of the first things John did in April 1813 was to join in the resolution to add another penny in the pound to the rate in order to fund three volunteers for the local militia, a pertinent reminder that the country was still at war and still in need of soldiers. The sum raised would pay the men a daily rate, but more importantly provide regular maintenance for their wives and families. Having served his time as an overseer, John was elected in 1815 to the higher office of churchwarden for the next two years, but when 1818 came, his attendance at the vestry meeting was recorded along with the 'inhabitants and occupiers' of the parish.

It was not in parish affairs alone that John was involved. He was making a name for himself in the town generally. The aftermath of the long and costly war against France, resolved at Waterloo, was felt as early as January 1816 when John, perhaps acting as spokesman for all the local brewers, published in *The Ipswich Journal* a copy of the letter he had sent to the government pleading for a reduction in the malt tax[8] which was affecting his business. He no doubt echoed the opinion of all those in whatever business when he complained of having to meet 'the present burthen of taxes, combined with no less oppressive parochial rates now called for, together with tradesmen's bills and other numerous ones, etc. Alas! How is the country to meet them from the great failure of rents & the universal want of money.'

That the economic situation was very serious indeed was reflected in the address given at the service of general Thanksgiving for the Restoration of Peace, which was held at the civic church of St Mary le Tower. The senior bailiff, William Batley, talked of the pressing need to find regular employment for the poor, the ranks of whom were now swollen by all the recently discharged soldiers and sailors. The Poor Rate levied on each parish throughout the country could not cope with the demands made upon it by those in need. Inevitably, the increase in poverty led to a sharp rise in crime as many of those without means or a settled address took to highway robbery, burglary and street muggings.

John eventually received a reply to his letter from the Chancellor of the Exchequer. This was passed to *The Ipswich Journal* for publication. The Chancellor wrote that 'public exigencies [not specified] will not admit of the duties on malt being taken off in the ensuing session but if such measures should be found practicable, provision would be made for returning the duty which may have been paid on stock in hand'. Unfortunately, we do not know what the reaction was of either John or the readers of the newspaper to this fine example of a political attempt to mollify civil unrest.

With the economic climate being so depressed, one would have thought that this was hardly the time to start a new business. We live in an age where we tend to consider ourselves more advanced than our predecessors of 200 years ago; where the young have far greater choice over what they should do with their lives and where we admire young entrepreneurs; but even in the first part of the twenty-first century it would be thought somewhat unusual for a young woman of 17, still technically regarded as a minor, to be mature enough to start her own business or even become a partner in one. Yet this is precisely what Eliza Acton did, when, on 30 March 1816, the following advertisement appeared in *The Ipswich Journal*:

Miss Nicholson and Miss Acton respectfully inform their Friends and the Public that on 2nd April next, they intend opening a Boarding School for Young Ladies at the pleasant and healthy village of Claydon, near Ipswich, where they will conduct a course of education, combining elegance and utility with economy.

Terms of the School (excluding washing)

Pupils under 8 years of age	16 guineas per annum
Eight and under 12	20 guineas per annum
Above 12	24 guineas per annum

The plan of instruction will include needlework, reading, writing, arithmetic, English grammar, geography, fancy-work, flower painting, the rudiments of the French tongue and music. If masters be required by the parents to attend the last accomplishments, the charges will be as usual.

No entrance, or other fees expected, and all extra charges sedulously avoided.

That Eliza had her parents' backing for this enterprise was shown in the addendum to the advertisement, which directed those requiring further information to call at the offices of Studd, Halliday & Acton rather than at the local printer's, as was more usual for replies to advertisements. Unfortunately, we know nothing at all of Miss Nicholson. We can make all sorts of assumptions; she and Eliza may have been very close friends who had for some time dreamed of opening their own school. Or she may have been somewhat older than Eliza, perhaps a mistress in the school Eliza attended, who had recognised the girl's potential to become a good teacher. Cynically one might surmise that having decided to open a school she asked Eliza to join her, gambling on the chance that John Acton was in a position to advance some of the capital needed to support the venture.

One can imagine the two women drawing up their business plan and giving careful thought to the wording of their promotional publicity. It was rare for such advertisements to publish all the terms of an establishment in such detail, so we may assume that having done their research, they decided to undercut similar schools. What is even more interesting is that some of the wording suggests that Eliza composed it, since it sums up the very philosophy she was to adopt in later life. In her cooking she was to combine elegance and utility with economy, hence her precise measurements, and 'all extra charges were to be sedulously avoided' was a practice that she would apply to the cost of the ingredients she recommended. Unfortunately, since the Overseers' Rate Books for Claydon have not survived, it has been impossible to trace the house in the village in which the school was situated. There remain several of the period that might fit the bill, including the rather austere flint-clad one that stands sideways on to the main road that some thirty or so years later housed the short-lived convent for an Anglican Sisterhood, supported by the fanatical High Church rector of the parish, the Reverend George Drury. It was a much gentler Revd Drury who was rector during Eliza's time in Claydon. We may imagine her lining up the girls on a Sunday morning for the walk to the parish church of St Peter, not as one might expect in the heart of the village, but set on high ground on a side road leading to the village of Akenham.

Since most pupils were boarders and went home only for short holidays at Christmas, Easter and the early summer, their lives, and those of their teachers, would have been very bound up with the village and its activities.

St Peter's church & the Gateway to Wolsey's College, Ipswich. (Engraving by Capone)

One can safely assume that visitors would have been welcome at any concerts or plays performed by the pupils, and in return the girls and the staff would have received invitations to Sales of Work undertaken by the ladies of the village, and other suitable entertainments at the homes or in the grounds of the wealthier residents. Their social sphere would not have been restricted to Claydon; there were also the adjoining parishes of Barham, with its great estate of Shrublands, and Great Blakenham; and just a bit further afield was the small country town of Needham Market. That Eliza was known in all these places is borne out later by those inhabitants who supported her as a poet.

It is frustrating that we have no means of knowing how successful the school was or how many pupils it attracted during the next four years, but in July 1820 it closed. On the 28th and 29th of that month an auction was held at the house in Claydon of 'the Household furniture and other effects of Miss Nicholson, declining her Seminary'. Included in the sale, along with a general assortment of articles, were 'fourteen new bedsteads with furniture, excellent feather mattresses, blankets, counterpanes, linen etc. tables, chairs, carpets, glass, earthenware, kitchen and culinary utensils'. If nothing else, unless the girls shared beds, we do know that pupil numbers did not exceed fourteen, which would have been quite a sizeable establishment for the time.

The press announcement states that it is Miss Nicholson who is 'declining' or giving up the school. So where was Eliza? Among the sparse biographical details that have been available to us in the past is the statement that Miss Acton had been taken ill the previous year and was sent abroad for the sake of her health. This, we now know, was not the case. Again, it is advertisements in *The Ipswich Journal* that provide the clues to the unexpected development in the story. One under the other on 11 September 1819 appear the following:

> The Misses Acton ... have taken a house at Great Bealings near Woodbridge where they intend opening an Establishment for a limited number of Young Ladies on 29th September.

And:

> Miss Acton being about to leave Claydon for Bealings, Miss Nicholson begs to inform her friends that it is her intention to continue her School in the former place.

So much for Eliza's ill health! She had left her former partner and gone into business with one or more of her sisters. This revelation opens up a whole new area of speculation. Had it been the intention right from the beginning that the sisters would one day have their own school and that Eliza's partnership with Miss Nicholson was, as it were, a training ground for the future while she waited for Anna and Catherine to be old enough to join her? In which case, was Miss Nicholson aware of the future plan or did it come as a complete surprise? Or had there been a falling out between them which led Eliza to suggest to her sisters that rather than their taking employment as governesses, they should try their luck with their own establishment? While it would fit a fictional

Picture of Woodbridge Town. (Attributed to Isaac Johnson (1754–1835))

narrative for Eliza and her former business partner to have parted on bad terms, it seems unlikely. Had Miss Nicholson felt aggrieved at being left in the lurch just before the beginning of term, surely she would not have mentioned in her advertisement the fact that Eliza was opening a rival establishment in Great Bealings.

What soon becomes apparent is that Miss Nicholson had found it hard to keep going. Possibly she had been unable to afford to replace Eliza as both teacher and business partner. From what we learn about Eliza in later life, it is certain that she must have been 'a born teacher'. She was young, lively and with so many younger sisters was used to dealing with girls. She knew

how to present lessons that were not only interesting but could also inspire young minds. Though she was herself still young, she commanded respect and admiration from the girls, so it may be that some of them defected to Eliza or that Miss Nicholson simply failed to attract new ones. Whatever the circumstances, she closed in 1820. As for the Miss Actons, all we know of their enterprise is that by 1822 they had moved from the village location in Great Bealings to premises in the busy thoroughfare in Woodbridge. This suggests that they were doing well and certainly four years later, when Eliza's book of poems was published, a number of her subscribers were resident in the Woodbridge area. And it is within the pages of the poetry book that we discover that some of her pupils were drawn from among the wealthier inhabitants. Among them was Sara Ellen Sharp, the motherless granddaughter of James Lynn MD, a renowned physician. Alas, he was unable to save the 13-year-old from a fatal illness but she lives on in the touching poem Eliza wrote following the girl's death.

While his daughters were spreading their wings and embarking on their teaching careers, it is clear that John had felt under financial pressure during 1816, which may account for why in November he felt it necessary to write to *The Ipswich Journal* about what surely should have been a personal matter:

having just heard a report from some respected friends, that a General Acton has lately died at Naples leaving a large property without any known heirs or claimants, I think it a duty I owe myself and family publicly to state I have the most perfect recollection of having heard my father and eldest brother say, more than twenty-five years ago and since, that we were related to a gentleman of the same name, residing at the Court of Naples in some official capacity, & that our Coat of Arms, consisting of lions and other things (I know not the terms of heraldry) were the same. I was only thirteen when my father died & death

& other incidental & unfortunate circumstances have lessened & separated the rest of our family. Since this, it has already been my fate to have earned, had given to and taken away from me, one fortune; other claims may perhaps be made; but should I be so fortunate as to have a just claim to heirship to and arrive at this, I trust it will be more stable, & enable me to fulfil the best wishes of my heart, that of providing, constituting & encreasing [sic] the comfort & happiness of my less fortunate fellow beings. I shall be thankful for any information upon the present subject & beg to state, I shall forthwith take every possible legal step to substantiate my claim, till those made convinced, being more nearly allied, have a superior right and title to the property.

J. Acton, St Peter's Brewery, Ipswich. 19 Nov. 1816.

Was John clutching at straws here in an attempt to reassure creditors that he might soon be financially stable? There seems to be little evidence that he was connected to Sir John Acton, who had distinguished himself by reorganising the Neapolitan Navy and later was the Prime Minister of Naples during the reign of Ferdinand IV. Those members of the English public who followed the gossip of the period would have heard mention of him through his encounters with Admiral Lord Nelson and Lady Hamilton, whose husband was English ambassador to the court of Naples. Sir John had died in 1811, leaving children. His brother, Joseph, who was a general and also in government service in Naples, did not die until 1830. Both brothers, the sons of a doctor, were born in Italy but were connected to the old Shropshire family of Actons which had retained its allegiance to the Catholic faith. Since nothing more was heard of the claim, we can only assume that John did not start on the long and expensive journey of seeking money that was held in Chancery, a process that we know from our reading of Dickens' novels[9] was often both soul-destroying and fruitless. As a solicitor, John should have known better than to embark on his suit, but perhaps the possibility of a fortune was too much temptation. If he did pursue the claim, that may have contributed to his later problems.

In the meantime he concentrated on business and family. That the country as a whole continued to suffer from economic depression manifested itself very close to home when, during the bitterly cold weather of February 1818, Studd, Halliday & Acton was robbed of eight

The 'Carnsey', 1886. 'Carnsey' was a dialect word to describe houses built on an embankment against flooding. (Sketch by Elizabeth Cotton, from the collection of A. Copsey)

bushels of coal – a relatively small amount, but a loss nonetheless. There seemed to be no way out of the deep recession and businesses of all types were closing down. Every week that year, the list of those countrywide who had been declared bankrupt filled two columns or more of both the local and national newspapers. To John, brewers and coal merchants seemed especially vulnerable, but shortage of cash and credit was no respecter of specific businesses.

It seemed there was just one disaster after another when in April, severe flooding in the area swept away the stone bridge which connected Dock Street with the town. Three men in the process of crossing the bridge were caught up in the swell. Prompt action by workmen from the brewery who threw ropes saved two of them, but the body of the third was not found for several days until it was washed ashore downstream. The problem of entry to and exit from the town was solved temporarily by making a bridge of boats strong enough to allow carriages across. Then for John Acton came another event, which at least took his mind off his financial problems for a day during that year. It was an episode that might well have turned into a family tragedy. His eldest son, Edward, had reached the age of 13. Growing up in a house full of women, Edward often sought peace and quiet by practising the gentle art of fishing from the banks of the River Gipping. One of his favourite spots was the millpond of Messrs Sheldrake and Welham not far from his home and it was there, one day during the July school holiday, that while Edward was casting his line from the bank, he saw a young boy in difficulty in the water. Quite how 8-year-old Jonathan Archer who could not swim came to fall in a pond that was between 10 and 15ft deep is not recorded, but for Edward, standing some 50 yards away, there was only one course of action. He stripped off his coat and waistcoat, dived into the water and brought the child, who had already sunk twice, to safety. The scene was witnessed and brought to the attention of the Ipswich Humane Society who recommended Edward for an award. The presentation of his medal took place in October and the president of the society, Milesom Edgar, spoke glowingly of Edward's unparalleled bravery. For the modern reader it may be of interest that young Jonathan was invited to attend the ceremony and after the presentation he and his grandmother were addressed by the president. The boy was warned against such behaviour that had endangered not only him but his saviour, too, while his grandmother was admonished for not keeping a better eye on the child.

As Lady Bracknell might have said, to save one body from drowning was heroic but to save another one looks like it was becoming a habit. It was eight years later in 1826 that Edward again became the talk of the town. At 14 he had gone off to spend two years at the grammar school in Bury St Edmunds where he had rounded off his education before becoming apprenticed to the surgeon Robert Carew King at Saxmundham. Now soon to celebrate his 21st birthday, his time with King was almost up and he would be leaving Suffolk to complete his medical training and gain his diploma at the South London Dispensary. On this second occasion Edward had jumped in the river to save a drowning soldier. *The Ipswich Journal* of 23 December stated:

> we have much pleasure in stating, that on Wednesday last, a handsome medal with an appropriate inscription thereon, expressive of the high regard the Humane Society entertained, of the intrepidity of Mr Edward Acton of this town, was presented to this young man, by Col. Edgar, president of the Society. The worthy chairman expressed himself in the most animated terms before the assembly and presented the token of esteem, with the heartfelt concurrence of the whole meeting.

The report continued that gratification had been added to the occasion by the presence of the young man whose life Edward had saved. Reading between the lines it would appear that for Private James Gleeson, life in the Army had proved too much and he had attempted suicide. Fortunately for him, after being saved he was not simply returned to his regiment to get on with his life. Living up to its name, the Humane Society had stepped in and used their funds to obtain his discharge from the Army and reunite him with his wife and family.

Edward's penchant for life saving continued and he was to prove a good doctor – or surgeon, as general practitioners were known then. He was to go into practice on his own far sooner than he had anticipated due to a family bereavement. In time he would marry and have a family, but to the end of his life he remained pivotal in the lives of his parents and sisters. As 1826 drew to a close he would soon discover that life was going to change greatly for all of them.

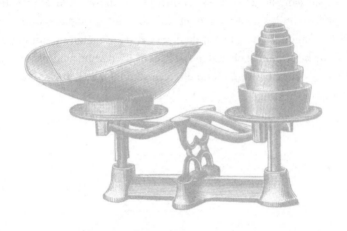

THREE

THE POET

[Her poetry is] romantic, derivative and often banal. The command of the cliché which she displays in her verse, is, happily, not repeated in her works on gastronomy.

First Catch Your Hare, Mary Aylett & Olive Ordish, Macdonald, 1965

It had been in 1822 that the Misses Acton removed their school from Great Bealings to Woodbridge. No further advertisements for it appeared in *The Ipswich Journal* but the Misses Actons' Academy is listed in *Pigot's Directory* of Suffolk for 1823–4. Probably the school did not exist for much longer after that. From various sources it appears that Eliza was active in the social life of Woodbridge and had a wide acquaintance among the local shopkeepers, professional men – attorneys and physicians – as well as what were termed the gentry, in particular their wives and daughters. From a delightful, handwritten unpublished poem, now housed in the British Library, we get a glimpse of the young woman who signed herself as a 'looker-on'. She describes a scene she had witnessed. The poem was sent to Mr William Whincopp, a gentleman of about 30, who may well have been a participant in the episode which depicts the female treatment of young men at its very worst. The poem shows great humour as well as critical understanding of both sexes. 'The Reception', as it was ironically titled, was obviously intended only for Mr Whincopp's pleasure; a private piece not meant for general perusal, which perhaps suggests they shared a close friendship. In style it is very different from much of her other

Portrait of Mr William Whincopp in his later years. (Sketch by Thomas Churchyard)

work, foreshadowing her later attempts to write dramatic pieces for the stage. It is too long to quote in full, but here are the opening lines:

Oh! tell me, who can those ladies be
Whom in their own abode I see,
Rowing, and sobbing, and stamping about,
And vowing they'll turn those gentlemen out?
Oh! Call them not ladies – for ladies I vow
Would ne'er in a passion like this be seen.
Their eyes flash forth such terrible slays
They're enough to set the house in a blaze;
Their voices are raised so loud, and high,
They almost resound to the vaulted sky;
The flush of anger is on their brow,
And louder and louder, they're scolding now,
And I hear them in tones terrific say
'I desire and insist that you go away,
For another instant you shall not stay.'
While those quiet young men sit still with dread,
And timidly listen to what is said
And scarcely venture a word to utter
And speak, but in a most gentle mutter,
And earnestly wish that each noisy dame,
Should lower her voice, and do the same.
Oh! what can they both have done amiss
To occasion them such a lecture as this?

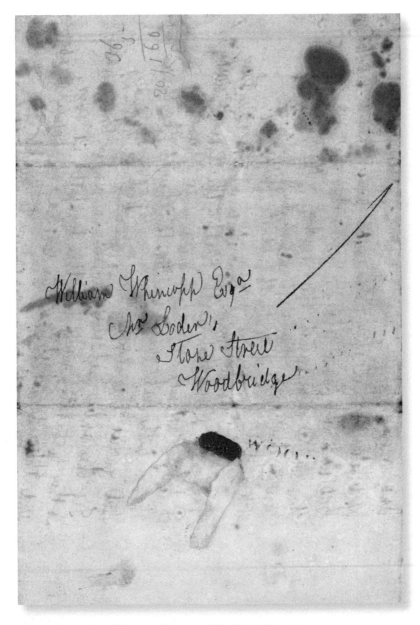

Addressed to William Whincopp. (Courtesy of The British Library)

The picture these lines conjure up could well have come straight out of Sheridan's *The Rivals*, where young ladies discuss the best way to treat a young man to gain his interest, while Jane Austen's readers could imagine that Lydia Bennett might have behaved in such a manner to the officers she flirted with in the shops in Meryton.[10] The poem goes on to explain that one of the two gentlemen involved had merely come to the house to borrow a book. Although a wine merchant by trade, who was probably known to the Acton girls through his business connection with their father, William Whincopp, like many young gentlemen of the period, had a very strong interest in geology, eventually becoming both an authority on and collector of fossils. His interest in archaeology was one he later shared with Eliza's brother Edward. Eliza addressed the poem to 'The most honourable William Whincopp' and had it sent or delivered to John Loder's Bookshop in the main street in Woodbridge, it being customary at that time for letters to be sent to shops to await collection. The use of the term 'honourable' was not a courtesy title to which William had a right, but suggests the easy familiarity which existed between them.

The very existence of this manuscript poem shows us how much the writing of poetry had become part of Eliza's life, making us question how many other such verses have been lost to us. It was in 1826 that we next hear of her, by which time she was staking her reputation as a poet by publishing a collection of her poetry. In the absence of other documentary contributions by her, is it possible that we can learn any more about her life from her writing? My old professor of English would pound his fist on his lectern as he urged us to look for the internal clues in a piece of writing, and surely of all the literary forms poetry is the one that reveals most about the author. So we need to search among the poems for what Eliza was doing in those missing years and perhaps, more importantly, for what she tells us about herself.

The sixty-one poems do not seem to be arranged in any particular order, either of subject matter or date of composition. Only five of them are actually dated, the first one in the volume bearing the date of December 1825. This, which is an elegy on the death of a gentleman whose home was close to the village of Claydon, would on first sight appear to be the latest in the collection, but when we get towards the end of the poems there is one dated as late as May 1826. In between there is the one, previously mentioned, dedicated to Ellen Sharp following her death in 1822,

The Reception.

A Poem.

Addressed to the most honourable
William Whincopp

Oh! tell me, who can these ladies be,
Whom in their own abode I see;
Raving, and scolding, and stamping about,
And vowing they'll turn these gentlemen out?
Oh! call them not ladies—for ladies I ween
Would ne'er in a passion like this be seen.
Their eyes flash forth such terrible rays,
They're enough to set the house in a blaze;
Their voices are raised so loud, and high,
They almost resound to the vaulted sky;
The flush of anger is on their brow;
And louder, and louder, they are scolding now;
And I hear them, in tones terrific, say,
"I desire and insist that you go away.
For another instant you shall not stay,"
While these quiet young men sit still with dread,
And timidly listen to what is said,
And scarcely venture a word to utter,
And speak, but in a most gentle mutter,
And earnestly wish that each noisy dame,
Would lower her voice, and do the same—
Oh! what can they both have done amiss
To occasion them such a lecture as this?

'The Reception', Eliza's unpublished poem in her own handwriting. (Courtesy of The British Library)

Why, the simple truth is this, you'll find,
That one, with a wish to improve his mind,
Came in, a most useful book to borrow,
Instead of which, he received, to his sorrow
A greeting, he ne'er would have come to meet;
He would rather have stay'd all night in the street,
Such was his errand — and then the other
Three in meekness at least, appeared his brother
Had come, with his gentle voice to say,
"Be guided by me to that better way,
Which leads to that glorious world of bliss,
Where the sorrows are all unknown of this;
Where joy is perfect, and bliss is pure,
And in changeless beauty, they ever endure."
And quite to excuse him from censure — he,
Comes in official capacity —
By the bishop's advice, he tries to please
His parishioners by such calls as these —
"Friendly, and proper, and good you see,
Was their purpose in coming as purposes would be,

another dated February 1824 for her sister Susannah and one entitled 'On Approaching Paris' which also bears the date of 1826 but gives no indication of it being written before or after the one to her mother. Earlier accounts of her life have recorded that Eliza went to France for the sake of health immediately after leaving Miss Nicholson in 1819. That, we now know, was not so but we can only conclude that it was probably in 1823 that she set out for the Continent. Again, we do not know if she really was suffering from something that required a change of climate or if she was taking the opportunity to do a scaled-down version of the Grand Tour of Europe that was so popular with both ladies and gentlemen who had begun flocking to the Continent once peace had been restored. If the latter then obviously she would not have travelled on her own, and as the family was not in a financial position to support her and a chaperone, we are offered two alternatives as to how and why she undertook the journey. The first is that she was asked, perhaps by the parents of a former pupil, to accompany them to France as a governess to one or more young lady. The second possibility is that she was taken as a lady's companion. Eliza had an aunt, Mrs Charlotte Miller, her mother's sister, a childless widow of independent means only twenty-two years older than Eliza, who lived in Kent. Had she wished to travel, then a suitable niece was just the person to have with her – and Eliza had the added advantage of speaking fluent French.

It was in October 1826 that *Poems by Eliza Acton* was printed and published by Richard Deck of Ipswich. At that time, a printer/publisher rarely risked his own money on an author, the demand for a new work being gauged by the number of subscribers who were willing to pay in advance for a copy. The fact that 328 copies of the *Poems*, at 5s each, were ordered prior to publication day shows that Eliza must already have made a name for herself locally as a promising young poet. It is likely that she had for some time contributed her work to magazines which published new poetry within their pages. The names and location of the subscribers appeared on pages ix–xxi, after the List of Contents. Fifty-eight lived either in the Maidstone area of Kent or East Farleigh, and a number of them can be identified as family members or friends of the Acton family. But the bulk of orders came from those living in Suffolk, among them a good cross-section of the nobility, gentry and clergy, as well as the more prosperous business people and civic leaders of Ipswich and the surrounding area. As one might expect, the ladies outnumbered the gentlemen, and in many cases individual members of a family bought separate copies. Eliza could name among her subscribers a viscount who lived in a castle, a lady living in Brussels and the Thayer brothers, who were resident in Paris and about whom we will hear later. Perhaps the most intriguing figure on the list was the Mr H. Potter whose address was given as St Helena, a place well known to the population of Britain at that time as being the island exile of Napoleon. It is likely that Potter was part of the British military establishment responsible for guarding the former French emperor. How or why did Mr Potter in St Helena come to order Eliza Acton's book in Suffolk? One answer could be that he was a brother of the John Potter who less than two years later would marry Eliza's sister, Anna.

Quite how the forthcoming edition was advertised is not clear. Certainly *The Ipswich Journal* did not carry any pre-publication advertisements for it, so we can only surmise that word was passed by recommendation and through the local libraries and bookshops. After Deck's name on the title page comes the following: 'sold also by Longman & Co. Paternoster Row, London; Deck, Bury; Cowell, Piper, and Shalders, Ipswich; Loder, Woodbridge; Hardacre, Hadleigh; Woolby, Stowmarket; and Stacy, Norwich.' The East Anglian connection was to be expected, but that Thomas Longman was willing to sell the book in London shows a certain confidence in the author that Eliza was later to exploit.

The book was so successful that within a month Deck had to do a reprint. We should perhaps pause here to remind ourselves that both the reading and writing of verse was much more common then than it is today. Eliza and her sisters would have been brought up on a diet of Shakespeare, Milton, Pope and Dryden. Added to these would have been the more recent poets, Thompson, Grey, Chatterton and Blake, followed by the Romantics: Wordsworth, Coleridge, Byron, Shelley and Keats, the last three all dying in the five years before Eliza's work appeared. But Suffolk had a fine poetic tradition of its own, the most famous being George Crabbe who, I suspect, had a strong influence on her work. Then there was Bernard Barton the Quaker poet, and Anne Candler, the Cottager poet, who wrote most of her poems during her twenty years of confinement in the House of Industry at Tattingstone, 6 miles from Ipswich. She, like other aspiring poets, found a vehicle for her work in the pages of *The Ipswich Journal*. Candler was fortunate that her work came to the attention of Mrs Elizabeth Cobbold, the Ipswich patroness who gave generous support to local talent. She undertook to edit Candler's work (not always to its advantage!) and she raised sufficient subscribers to support the printing of Candler's collected works in 1802. The response was such that the Cottager poet, as she became known, was able to leave the workhouse and live in reasonable comfort until her death in 1814. But not all those who sent their poetic offerings to the newspaper were talented. That the standard was variable is apparent in the review of Eliza's book that appeared in *The Ipswich Journal* on 21 October 1826:

> It is always with pain, that we deem ourselves called upon as Public Journalists to wound with the caustic pen of criticism, the feelings of the young and ardent aspirant of poetical fame, and in the same proportion that we feel this distinction to wound, we avail ourselves with eager haste, to offer our meed of applause where it is justly merited.

An opportunity of indulging these last kindlier dictates of a judgement is now afforded us, in recommending to the perusal of our readers, a neat elegant volume of Poems, just published by Miss Eliza Acton of this town. Throughout the whole is breathed a spirit of poesy, which we often look for in vain in the production of those 'more known to Fame' ...

(Perhaps the reviewer had in mind such an offering as that in 1810 from a long-forgotten Poet Laureate, H.J. Pipe.[11] Entitled 'Ode for the New Year', it begins thus:

> 'Ere yet, mid Rhedecyna's bowers
> I humbly cull'd the Muse's flowers
> By silver Isis' sedgy side.
> Not rolling there a classic tide,
> My native meads and groves among
>   As blythe I tun'd my artless song,
> My fancy hail'd the halcyon day
> Crown'd with our Sovreign's opening sway
> And pour'd the verse to that auspicious morn
> Which plac'd on Britain's throne a Monarch British born ...)

The journalist reviewer continued:

... and we are quite assured that if any of our friends follow our recommendment [sic] by perusing these poems, they will give testimony to the correctness of our opinion. We have only room for one short extract, which we accidentally selected, but which may be taken for a fair specimen of the young poet's talents.

> *Stanzas*
> I love in loneliness to stand afar,
> When lingering twilight gently rests around;
> And night is flinging from her 'ebon car'
> O'er earth, a shade more deep, and more profound;
> While one sweet star, – a solitary gem,
> Sparkleth in Ev'ning's dark'ning diadem!

Not long alone! – for soon, with gradual glow,
A thousand diamond-lights their fires disclose,
And on the beautiful and radiant brow
Of heav'n, in rich resplendency repose:
Yet still the first is fairest – and its beam
Smiles like some young enthusiast's early dream!

The following week, 28 October, on the front page of the newspaper appeared another review with examples of 'Cards of Fortune', with the footnote: 'These cards are designed to be formed into a pack, for the amusement of an evening circle. [E.A.].'[12] These thirty short verses completed the volume and on 25 November a notice appeared to the effect that the book had gone into a second edition.

So what did the subscribers find in the elegant volume? Probably the foregoing is the least representative of her work and is, I would suggest, an early piece. However, what was to become almost a trademark throughout her verse occurs in the first two lines, that is, her pleasure in being alone to enjoy twilight and the onset of night. The majority of her work avoids the excesses of such phrases as 'ebon car' and 'sparkleth in Ev'ning's dark'ning diadem'. There are poems such as one might expect from a young woman; the praise of nature and the seasons; the personal verses written for inclusion in a friend's album; and those mourning a death such as the opening poem, dated 15 December 1825, entitled 'On the Death of Major Whitefoord'. Sir John and Lady Whitefoord lived in Bramford Hall, in the village next to Claydon where Eliza had had her school. For several generations, Bramford Hall had been the family seat of the Actons, the family Eliza's father still liked to believe they belonged to. Eliza would certainly have known of the Whitefoords and evidence suggests that she was acquainted with Miss Whitefoord, who ordered a copy of the *Poems* from Brussels. This piece is very much one written especially for an occasion. If Eliza was living in France at the time, she would have had to rely on letters from home and the local newspaper reports for details of the accident that caused the major's death, but as we shall see later, it is more likely that she was back in Ipswich on a visit and this poem was a spontaneous response to the news of the death. An officer for twenty-three years in the 15th Hussars, Captain Whitefoord, as he then was, had fought at Waterloo where he had been wounded. His bravery earned him the rank of major, but since the bullet with which he had been hit was never removed, he was eventually forced to retire from active service. On the morning of 15 December, the major and his friend, Henry Franklyn, went out across the meadows from Bramford Hall to shoot snipe. The major was about three feet ahead of Franklyn, who had just loaded his gun ready to aim at a bird, when Franklyn's foot slipped as he stepped over a patch of water. Unable to steady himself he went down on his knees and in so doing his gun went off, discharging its entire contents into the back of his friend. The servants who accompanied the gentlemen carried the injured man to the nearest house and then back to the Hall, while the distraught Franklyn mounted the shooting pony and rode to Ipswich to fetch a surgeon. Sadly, the major's wounds proved fatal and within two hours he was dead. Eliza captures the atmosphere of the day in the opening line: 'Like blighted leaves, around us fall / The young, the gifted, and the brave; / And still the most belov'd of all / Seem earliest fated to the grave.'

Although she was able to write movingly for such an occasion, this is a piece that is controlled. It is what one might expect from a female writer of the period. What was perhaps totally unexpected from a young woman was the almost masculine intensity and depth of feeling that she expresses in many of her other poems. Women were not expected to experience, and certainly not publicly express, such overwhelming passion as that which could lead a young woman to worship the man she loves to the exclusion of her God, as Eliza does in 'Gertrude'. But she must have evoked many of her readers' deepest emotions as she describes both accurately and acutely the desperation and despair felt when a love affair ends, the deep depression which illness (or a broken heart) brings, and the longing for death that these states induce. Many young women experienced the pangs of disappointed or unrequited love, the failure of a relationship or the death of a loved one, but few female poets at that time were able to convey just how it felt.

It is difficult when reading the *Poems* to remember that Eliza was barely 26 when the volume was published, and that many of the sixty-one poems contained in it must have been written when she was considerably younger. Six are dedicated by name to her sisters and close friends. These came under a heading of 'Rhymes Written in Albums' and were intended to be included in the autograph albums of the young ladies concerned, as was a custom of the period that lingered well into the mid-twentieth century, though in somewhat less poetic form. Another bore the somewhat strange title of 'To a Friend, with a Pyrus Japonica'. One critic seems to have missed the comma, interpreting the verses as being dedicated to someone in possession of the Japonica rather than it being sent as a present. The flower, which sometimes blooms in the dark days of winter or very early in the spring, is being sent as a promise of the brighter days to come.

Most frustrating are the poems that are simply entitled 'To ******', thus hiding the identity of the people for whom they were intended. As one reads these it soon becomes apparent that some are intended for, or are about, the man she loved – the unknown, supposedly French officer to whom she was said to be engaged. We do not know either how or where she met him, or the length of their attachment. It is possible that he came from an émigré family and that he joined the English Army to fight against Napoleon. In which case, Eliza may have met him while he was stationed in Ipswich when she was very young or later in Woodbridge, the other local garrison town. It seems much more likely, however, that he was a member of the French Army and that they met in France.

The poems leave no doubt that she not only loved him deeply, but also admired him greatly. He was everything a young woman yearned for: handsome; of good breeding (there is a suggestion he came from a noble family); he had a beautiful voice and his smile melted her heart; and while he had the ability to command, he also possessed a gentleness of manner. He was, in her eyes and words, 'godlike'. In 'Song', she tells us more: 'Thou shalt know my love by his eagle-eye, / And his lofty brow, / Where in richness the dark curls clust'ring lie / On the forehead's snow!' and 'Brightest, mid all that is lordly, and gay; / Dauntless, and first, in the deadliest fray; / Graceful, and gifted, all others above, / Such shalt thou find him – my own gallant love.'

'To ******' expresses how she felt in the early days of their affair, when constantly throughout her waking hours when they were apart, the tiniest pleasant thing would remind her of him. 'How sacred is the lightest thing / Which wakes a thought of thee.' And as the day wore on, when 'Soft tones of music floating far / At ev'ning o'er the sea', and all was calm and serene, then she could look forward to 'but sweet dreams are / Which lead my soul to thee'.

On a number of occasions during their courtship he has to leave her to attend to official duties. In 'Le Triste Adieu' we learn of her fears at these partings. In answer to his accusation that she has grown cold towards him, she declares that he wrongs her and, addressing him as 'dearest', she assures him that 'There is no joy on earth to me / Where thou art not, – I sigh to hear / That voice of tend'rest melody / Still breathe its sweetness to mine ear.' Neither need he have any doubts of her faithfulness: 'words from other lips than thine / Pass, like the winds, unheeded by.' Theirs has been a long courtship and she hints that her health is suffering, but her main concern is that he may find it difficult to remain faithful to her once he is 'In Pleasure's halls, a welcome guest, / Thou wilt be courted, and carest, / And smil'd on by the loveliest.' There are a number of references throughout the poems to his becoming part of a social elite from which she is excluded; a circle that is shallow and fraught with temptation. Is it too much to suggest that this might well have been the re-established royal court?

Eliza's fears were justified, as we learn from 'L'Abandonnée':

> They said, the words I lov'd to hear
> Were whisper'd in another's ear,
> With that sweet smile, and tender tone,
> With which thou mad'st my heart thine own,
> I listen'd to the torturing tale,
> With brow and cheek as marble pale;
> Yet nerv'd I then my woman's soul,
> Its deadliest feelings to controul,
> And mov'd about as pale and wan,
> As if my very life were gone,
> And I a wand'ring spirit, left
> On earth, of ev'n a tomb bereft.

Can there be anyone, woman or man, who has been deserted for another, who does not identify with the feelings she expresses here; the attempt to remain in control and not show any outward emotion while inside one is totally numb, empty like the wandering spirit left on earth? The poem continues with her declaration that she would have given up everything for him, happy to share his name regardless of his position in life. She describes briefly the agony she has endured, but then, to make matters worse: 'And now thou com'st, thy wav'rings o'er, / To bid me be thy slave once more!' Again, how many of her readers would have empathised with this situation of a philanderer asking to be taken back? Will she, won't she?

> 'Tis vainly ask'd! – affection's chain
> Was all too rudely wrench'd in twain
> And never will unite again.
> That voice whose ev'ry accent fell
> Like softest music on mine ear,
> Hath lost its deep, its touching spell,
> Of eloquence unspeakable,
> Which was, in days gone by, so dear,
> I see thee with unthrobbing breast;
> I meet thy glance, yet still am calm,
> Go, then! – nor break the tranquil rest,
> Which is my spirit's needful balm.
> Leave me to peace! – my heart is grown,
> Since thou didst cast its love away,
> As cold, and careless as thine own,
> And might as soon its trust betray. –
> Yet, though estrang'd, upon the past
> Ev'n now unmov'd I cannot dwell:–
> My first affections, and my last,
> Were thine – thine only – fare thee well!

At this point, although she has resolutely rejected him, the final phrase shows that because of their shared past she is not just saying goodbye, she wishes him well in the future. In 'Yes! Leave Me' she says she is calm: 'I do not weep! – fast tears may fall / O'er transient cares, and lighter ill; / But oh! the bitterest griefs of all, / Are nurs'd in tearless anguish still.' She then reveals that she has always feared that his love would be transient. 'E'en in our happiest days I felt / Thy love was but a summer-beam', and now she knows 'that round that wand'ring heart / new ties are woven'. Running through all the poems which deal with the break-up of the relationship, there is a hint that the young man has done more than simply flirt with another woman. There is a clue in 'L'Abandonée' in the lines: 'I would have gladly borne for thee / Pain, – scorn, reproach – and penury; / Or, – dear as was thine early fame, / Have shar'd with thee a blighted name.'

In the self-explanatory 'Take Back thy Ring', she says he will falsely accuse her of being unable to face up to misfortune when the truth is that:

> Past years of deep devotedness,
> The fonder – truer – tale will tell
> Of my soul's changeless tenderness –
>
> And aught but this I could have borne –
> To know thee vile Dishonour's slave;
> The finger-mark of shame and scorn,
> Th' oppressor of the pure and brave.
>
> But never shall my fate be twin'd
> With that of one, whose fame is blasted;
> Whose word is as the idle wind;
> Whose days in servile guilt are wasted.

This theme of some ignominy attached to him is continued in 'It Were Dishonouring Now': 'It were dishonouring now – or I / Could weep in hopeless misery, / O'er the dark tale, which links thy name / To perfidy, and deepest shame.' She vows she will not give a thought to him:

> Whose nobleness and truth are gone!
> And 'tis enough for me to know,
> That crime hath track'd thy steps, – that thou
> Hast o'er the young and happy, shed,
> The curse which withers life away,
> And left, for fame and virtue fled,
> Remorse, and wretchedness to stay.

He had come 'like a spoiler' to break hearts, 'which bled too late / And early years made desolate, / Have been thy fatal gifts to those, / Who dar'd upon thy faith repose. / Reproach is not for me! Thy doom, / Without it is o'er fraught with gloom, / And grief, and bitterness.' Whatever it is he has done cannot be forgiven, despite misleading us with 'Forgive Thee! – Yes'. She qualifies the answer by suggesting that forgiveness will come in time – at her death, when she has erased from her memory his voice and smile, and 'when each hope is rais'd to heav'n, / Which with'red in the world's cold shade; / And thou – e'en thou – shalt be forgiven / The wretchedness which thou hast made.'

An emphasis has been placed upon looking at the poems which deal with the love affair in an attempt to learn something about the man concerned, but it must not be supposed that all the sixty-one verses in the volume are as intense as those quoted. Sixty-one, surely a strange number, suggests that one may have been inserted at the last moment. When selecting the work to be included, Eliza chose a number of different styles and themes, from the gentle invocations to the night to deep musings upon philosophical ideas. Perhaps the most surprising of all her poems is the forty-five lines of blank verse entitled 'A Sketch'. It was not the first time that a painting or drawing had inspired her to write. The simply titled 'Portrait', although the first two lines curiously have not been printed, describes a Classical picture, seen perhaps during her visit to Venice. But 'A Sketch' is very different. It begins:

> Where is he now? – that mightiest one, whose name
> Was still the spell-word of the fray, – the sound
> Which led his legions on untir'd, to win
> Their thousand fights; – the man whose daring deeds
> Were heralded by Fame, till Fame herself
> Exhausted sank beneath th' o'erwhelming task.
> And is his high career of glory done? –
> Can he be nothing, to whom monarchs bow'd
> Their crown-encircled brows, and nations knelt
> In most subservient homage, till he stood
> E'en like a god above the conquer'd world?
> Where is he now? – Far o'er the rolling waves,
> On a most rude, and sea-surrounded rock,
> Rises a simple tomb, whose whiteness gleams
> Through the low-bending branches of the tree,

> Which droops, in seeming mournfulness, above
> The marble monument it shadows o'er
> 'Tis there an emperor sleeps! And on that isle
> Which his foes made his dwelling-place, he pin'd
> Like a cag'd eagle, till he perished there.

It is a shock to realise that this is about Napoleon, to whom she, an Englishwoman, appears to show sympathy. There were, of course, many Englishmen who admired him and supported his ideas of reform, if not his lust for power. But Eliza is not just empathising with the man in exile, she is examining the question of how power corrupts and how quickly those at the top can be brought down. 'Pois'd on the proudest pinnacle of pow'r, / He fell, as doth the breath-stirr'd avalanche, / With fearful, and appalling suddenness.' But while accepting that Napoleon 'was our enemy! – he had been / The scourge of human-kind – and for this / His blood had been required', she did not believe that it was right to incarcerate him on St Helena for the rest of his life. His vanquishers would have shown greater generosity if they had demanded his death: 'and if for this / His blood had been required, they had done well / To shed it quickly; not to drain his life / By slow sure means ...'

Since Napoleon had died in 1821 we know this poem must have been written some time after that. It would seem to date from the period when she was living in France and mixing with those whose sympathies lay with Bonaparte. Which brings us back to the two brothers, Amédée and Edward Thayer, who subscribed to Eliza's poetry book. Their father was a Gloucestershire businessman who at the beginning of the French Revolution had gone to Paris seeking compensation for the cargo of one of his brothers' ships, which the French government had seized. Staying longer than he had anticipated and then marrying, he found that there was money to be made in buying from the government the confiscated property of those wealthy citizens who had either been executed or managed to escape as émigrés to England. He also had the foresight to buy the patent rights to Robert Fulton's Panorama[13] and then set about building such a spectacle in the Montmartre property he had bought. Property dealing and further panoramas, including the one suggested by Napoleon in 1809, made him a very wealthy man. His two sons were born in 1799 and 1802. When

The Tomb of Napoleon in St Helena. (Pencil drawing by Charles Harry Roberts, National Library of Australia)

Eliza knew them, for surely she must have done if they became subscribers to her book, they were both unmarried, although Amédée may already have been engaged to Hortense Bertrand, whom he married in May 1828. Hortense, who was the daughter of General Bertrand, had accompanied her father to St Helena with Napoleon. An extract from a diary of W.I. Hopkins of Rhode Island, USA, provides first-hand information:

April 23rd 1837. I dined at Madame [Edward] Thayer's, rue de Menars. There were fifteen or twenty guests, the Duke of Padua; an officer of the British Army and his wife; a Colonel in the French Army ... a French Captain and several others were there. I was placed at the table between the Duke of Padua and Madame Amédée Thayer, who is the daughter of General Bertrand and was at Saint Helena with Bonaparte. She was one of the most beautiful women I have seen in France, although thin and pale from the effects of long illness. She speaks English as well as I do and conversed with me with a frankness and amiability which left nothing to be desired. She said that her recollections of St Helena and of Bonaparte are very vivid although it is sixteen years since she came from there. She spoke of enjoying herself there greatly and said she would even be willing to return ...

If Hortense's memories were still sharp after sixteen years, how much clearer they must have been around 1825/6. Was it she who showed Eliza the sketch of the simple white tomb seen through the trees and regaled her with stories of life on St Helena? Certainly she can have left no doubt of her allegiance to Bonaparte when she named her first child, a son, Napoleon. (He died at the age of 12, while a second son died in his second year and the third at birth.) That Amédée shared his wife's enthusiasm for the late emperor is borne out by a further eyewitness account of a large cabinet filled with Napoleonic relics that stood in one of the rooms of their home. Both brothers later became senators and both were known for their great generosity to the poor. It is tempting to think that Eliza met the Thayer brothers through her faithless lover, but a much more prosaic answer has been suggested which takes us right back to Eliza's time in Claydon. Among the list of subscribers were three with the surname Beck, including two doctors; one in Ipswich and another with a large family in Needham Market. The third subscriber was a Mrs Beck who lived in nearby Creeting. It turns out that Mrs Thayer, the mother of Amédée and Edward, was born Harriet Beck in Suffolk in 1770. If she was indeed related to the Needham Market family, then what could have been more natural when they discovered that Eliza was going to Paris than that they should give her an introduction to Mrs Thayer and the rest of their French relations?

Today's readers may find Eliza's emphasis on mortality morbid, but to a nineteenth-century audience death was an ever-present reality. At a time when diseases such as cholera and tuberculosis were prevalent, one became accustomed to hearing of the sudden demise of a young person or watching with dread the slow decline of a friend or family member. In her worst moments of depression Eliza looks forward to her own death. In many of the poems, the sickness she refers to appears to be attributed to her broken heart, but at other times she hints that there has been a shadow overhanging her from childhood, perhaps some lingering condition likely to hasten an early death.

That the poems were not placed in any chronological order is clear, since placed at number twenty-six is 'On Approaching Paris'. This is one of the few that bears a date, not a specific one, merely 1826. I suggest that this predates the valedictory 'Lines Written Abroad', which is dated May 1826. It seems more than likely that Eliza had been in England towards the end of 1825 for several months and that she returned to Paris in April or early May, five months before her poetry book was published in October of that year. The opening of 'Lines Written Abroad' states: 'I have but left my pleasant home / And native vales, to die.' The word 'but' can mean 'just' or 'recently', indicating the visit home. 'Je vais te quitter ségour aimé' (I am going to leave you, the place I love) describes her farewell to her home:

> My quiet home, farewell! I go –
> Forth to the cold bleak world again,
> A wanderer mid its scenes of woe,
> To seek for sheltering peace in vain.
> Oh! long my heart will warmly cling
> To thee, as to some hallow'd spot,
> Where falsehood's deadly withering,
> And life's stern storms were all forgot.
> ...
> My cherish'd home a long farewell!

It was while she was at home in Ipswich with her family that she must have made arrangements for the publication of her work. Did she, perhaps, consider that the volume might even be a posthumous one? And was it this final poem, which might be called a letter to her mother, which was squeezed into the folio and became poem number sixty-one?

> My Mother! – thou wilt hope in vain,
> Thy wandering one's return; –
> 'Twould calm the bitterness of pain,
> If once on thy dear face again
> My parting glance might return.
> But sever'd thus by land, and wave,
> From tenderness, and thee,
> And all whose love, might sooth, or save,

I perish here – and ev'n my grave

In stranger-earth must be!

But, fearful though she was, Eliza did not die. Which brings us to the vexed question of the piece of gossip which has dogged Eliza's footsteps certainly since the publication of Aylett and Ordish's book *First Catch Your Hare* in 1965. According to the authors, Eliza gave birth to a daughter in 1826. The source of this information was a great-niece of the daughter who was apparently named Susanna. It was believed that the baby was absorbed into the family of one of Eliza's two sisters, Sarah and Susannah. As so often happens with stories passed down through families, things can get somewhat distorted with time. As we know, Eliza had several sisters only one of whom was named Susannah, and she never married. In fact, in 1826 none of the Acton girls was married. However, Aylett and Ordish relate that the sister Sarah married a Joseph Heskins who, when Sarah died, later married the other sister. What is interesting is that a relation of Eliza, possibly an aunt or a cousin, one Mary Ann Mercer, did marry a Joseph Heskins, a commercial traveller at St Olave's, Hart Street, City of London, in 1808, and that he did marry Susannah Mercer on the death of his wife. Aylett's informant pointed out that the family had always questioned the legality of the second marriage because, according to the Table of Affinity, it was against the law to marry one's sister or brother-in-law. There is no baptismal record for the baby; neither does she appear in any census under the name of Heskins. The final pieces of evidence given to Aylett and Ordish were that it was known in the family that the child Susanna was in receipt of a private allowance and that she was reputed to have a portrait of Eliza, which she regularly kissed stating that this was her real mother. I wish I had been able to meet members of the family to verify these stories for myself. However, although a Mr and Mrs Heskins of Chertsey were subscribers to the *Poems*, a detailed analysis of their family tree does not reveal a child who might fit the bill as Eliza's daughter.

If indeed Eliza did have a child in 1826, it was presumably some time after her return to France in May. And if she did, it was most likely that the child would have been placed with foster parents. Among the middle classes and the aristocracy, it was quite usual for young ladies who found themselves pregnant to be sent to live either in retirement in the country or abroad where they were unknown until after the birth, and then a home was found for the child. London abounded with private 'homes for lying-in' for young ladies, and novels by Jane Austen, Charles Dickens and Charlotte Brontë all tackled the subject of illegitimate children.

If 'The Reception' dates from the early 1820s, Eliza's last known poem was dated 1842. In that year Richard & John E. Taylor, printers and publishers of Red Lion Court, Fleet Street in London, produced a small volume bound in green silk with a raised floral pattern of the eight-stanza poem entitled 'The Voice of the North'. The world had moved on since the 1820s. The reigns of the Georges were over, as was that of the elderly William IV, and in their place was a young queen who had recently married Albert, Duke of Saxe-Coburg-Gotha. In 1842 they were expected to make their first visit to the most northerly realm of the kingdom, and this poem was intended to express the joyful anticipation of the Scots to welcome their sovereign. The poem is very much a set piece intended for the mass market, a tiny keepsake for the occasion, of somewhat better quality than the modern royal souvenir of mug or tea towel. One has to question why the publishers did not commission a native Scot to extol the virtues of the country rather than someone who, as far as we can tell, had never visited Scotland. Was it that Eliza's reputation was high or did she approach the Taylors with the ready-made poem, the tone of which is decidedly sycophantic and almost deserves the label of banal:

> God speed thee, gracious Lady!
> God speed thee to the strand
> Where million loving hearts await
> The Queen of all the land;
> Who comes in her young beauty
> From bonny England forth,
> With her own sweet smile to gladden
> The children of the North.

In the second stanza she mentions Prince Albert, 'Gotha's princely son / The noble and the true – who well / Deserves the bliss he won.' During the rest of the poem she mentions fragrant heather, bending harebells, and forest haunts, 'where the red deer roameth free'. For the benefit of those who knew nothing of Scotland, we are also treated to descriptions of the scenery: crags and glens and waterfalls, mountains topped with snow and gleaming lakes. Those same stirrings of strong emotion, produced by the sound of the pibroch or martial bagpipe, will be felt by the Scots when they behold the queen.

> Then haste thee, sweetest Lady!
> Oh haste thee to the strand,
> Where million loving hearts await
> The Queen of all the land,
> Who comes in her young beauty
> From bonny England forth,
> With her rejoicing smile to glad
> The Children of the North.

Perhaps it is because this was an occasional piece that Eliza seems to lose both her spontaneity and passion. Maybe, with age, she no longer felt as intensely as she once had, or was it that she recognised that with changing times, her type of poetry was no longer either fashionable or in demand?

Among her circle of literary and artistic acquaintances was Frances Maria Kelly. Miss Kelly, who came from a theatrical background, was an actress who had a mission to make the theatre and the acting profession accessible, and to that end she rented premises in Dean Street in London's Soho, where in 1840 she opened a Theatre and Dramatic School. A very independent woman, she counted both Dickens and Charles Lamb among her friends. Lamb was reputed to have been in love with her and proposed marriage, which she rejected. It is believed that Mary Ellen Greville, who lived with her and is recorded in the censuses of the time as her 'god daughter', was in fact her natural child, born in Edinburgh around 1829. Frances Kelly's relevance in Eliza's story is that a play written by Eliza was reputed to have been produced by Frances in her new theatre, some time after May 1840. No record of this remains, but is it possible that with the passage of time, the history of the two women has become entangled and this is in fact where the story of Eliza's child comes from?

FOUR

DISASTER AND CHANGE

T wo very dissimilar items that appeared in the press in the autumn of 1826 show that economic affairs had still not improved nationwide. The first was that two members of the royal family, Her Majesty the Queen Dowager of Württemberg (the Princess Royal of England) and her sister, both of whom were residing outside the country, had sent considerable donations to England for the relief of distressed manufacturers. At a more parochial level, in Ipswich Samuel Burrows, a pawnbroker, advertised an auction of unredeemed pledges. The variety of goods on offer showed only too clearly that hardship was not confined to the very poor. Mr Burrows had silver-plated goods with a combined weight of 178 ounces, as well as seven gold watches and thirty silver ones. He did not even bother to elaborate on the various items of both ladies' and gentlemen's jewellery, or the number of guns and pistols he held, or the assortment of prints, paintings, china and glass that were to be disposed of, all of which suggest that the original owners had at one time been affluent. More distressing were the articles of clothing, bedding and household items which spoke of desperation. Even the Ipswich Public Library, which was housed in Mr Raw, the bookseller and printer's establishment in the Buttermarket, was considering if the guinea joining fee for new subscribers should be dropped, presumably because membership had fallen off. But there was some good news for hard-pressed book-buyers; Edward Hunt, bookseller and stationer of Tavern Street, 'begged to apprize the Public that from the <u>very stagnated</u>

[sic] situation of the Market he had purchased an extensive collection of books underpriced'. Examples included Hogarth's Works at £20.00, reduced from the publisher's price of £32 12s 0d. His advertisement, which gave a lengthy list of books with both retail and reduced prices, showed just how expensive books were at that period.

The first hint that John Acton was in real trouble was an announcement that appeared on 29 April 1826. Under the heading 'Studd, Halliday & Acton', it read:

> An advertisement having appeared in the Ipswich Papers of last week, signed by Pearson & Lawrence stating that the Partnership of the above firm was dissolved on 25 March last I hereby declare that such an Advertisement was inserted without my knowledge or consent and I am entirely ignorant of any legal Dissolution having taken place.
> Signed John Acton.

This surely was an unusual move, but it suggests that John's relationship with Halliday and Mrs Studd had deteriorated. However, nothing further appeared on the subject and by October Eliza Acton's name had replaced her father's, as Edward's would in December. There was no hint then that within days of Edward's medal ceremony, the Acton family would sever its quarter-century link with the town.

Had others known that John was having more business worries than usual? Or did it come as a complete shock to the local inhabitants when on 13 January 1827 the advertisement appeared announcing the sale of the Actons' household furniture? From all the items mentioned in an earlier chapter it would appear that everything, apart from purely personal belongings, was offered for sale. Was John aware of the irony of this situation? Ten years earlier he had said in that very public letter explaining his attempted claim on the estate of General Acton of Naples, that 'he had earned, been given and had taken from him a fortune', and now the same thing was happening all over again. Just as his dead father had left instructions for all his goods and chattels to be sold, so now a living John was doing something very similar to his family. In advertisements for the sale of house contents at that time, it was usual to give a reason for it taking place, such as the death of the owner or removal to another address. More frequently a declaration of bankruptcy could have been the cause. However, this particular notice revealed nothing beyond the list of items on offer.

Those who were in any doubt as to why the Actons seemed to have disappeared so suddenly, or wondered where they had gone, had to wait some eleven months to find out from the *London Gazette* of 20 November 1827:

> Whereas a Commissioner of Bankrupt is awarded and issued forth against John Acton, late of Ipswich, in the County of Suffolk, Beer-Brewer, Maltster, Wine and Spirit and Corn and Coal Merchant, Dealer and Chapman[14] (late Partner with Simon Halliday and Mary Studd, at Ipswich, aforesaid, trading under the firm of Studd, Halliday and Acton, lately residing at Calais, in the kingdom of France, and now remaining abroad) and he being declared a bankrupt is hereby required to surrender himself to the Commissioners in the said Commission named, or the major part of them on the 27th of November instant, at Eleven in the forenoon; on the 4th December next and on the 1st of January following at ten o'clock in the Forenoon, at the Court Commissioners of Bankrupts, in Basinghall-Street, in the City of London, and make a full discovery and disclosure of his estate and effects; when and where the Creditors are to come prepared to prove their debts, and at the second sitting to choose an Assignee or Assignees, and at the last sitting the said Bankrupt is required to finish his examination. All persons indebted to the said Bankrupt, or that have any of his effects, are not to pay or deliver the same but to whom the Commissioners shall appoint, but give notice to Messrs Norton and Chaplin, Solicitors, 3 Gray's Inn Square, London.

Bankruptcy was an ever-present hazard for anyone engaged in business. Every week *The Ipswich Journal* published details of those who could no longer carry on their trade or profession because the debts they had accrued had mounted to such a peak that they could no longer be paid in full, if at all. The usual procedure was for those to whom money was owed to apply to the courts for the assets of the debtor to be seized and sold in order that the creditors might receive at least a moiety of what was owed them. Those whose assets could in no way repay their creditors were usually arrested and imprisoned. Charles Dickens' *Little Dorrit* offers a picture of what life was like for the debtor and his family in a debtors' prison in London. But there were no such separate institutions as the Fleet or the Marshalsea in provincial towns, where debtors were housed in the town gaol along with common criminals. Such would have been John's fate had he not taken the route followed by many other insolvents, among them Nelson's mistress Emma Hamilton – to put himself into voluntary exile in France and so evade capture.

So he failed to appear in London before the commissioners on the three dates specified. Notices were posted again on 4 and 21 December detailing adjournment dates for his examination. On 8 January 1828 an order was made by the Lord High Chancellor granting him extra time 'to surrender himself and make full discovery and disclosure of his estate and effects'. He was given forty-nine days' grace dating from 1 January and was then expected to appear before the commissioners on 19 February between 11 a.m. and 1 p.m. to finish his examination. *The Ipswich Journal* of 26 January 1828 furnished details, which were not quite so bogged down in official language, of the petition that was lodged on John's behalf. It appeared that it was indeed Simon Halliday, his former partner, who had sued him for bankruptcy. John's solicitors, Rose and Knight, argued on his behalf that firstly he had not committed an act of bankruptcy, and secondly on the technical point that the debt he owed Mr Halliday was on bonds, not a good petitioning creditor's debt since no final settlement of the partnership affairs had taken place. The vice chancellor, having listened to these arguments and those by Mr Halliday's lawyers, Sugden & Rolfe, gave his judgement on 11 January. In doing so, he cast doubt on John's credibility by commenting on details which, unfortunately, were not revealed. But at the same time he did disclose one fact that is important in our story:

His Honour said it appeared to him that Mr Acton must have stated things in his affidavits which he knew were untrue. It appeared to him there was a sufficient act of bankruptcy. He thought it clear that Acton did not go abroad to see this daughter who was ill at Paris; there was not even an allegation that he ever did see her but he was at Calais on the last day of December 1826, and on the 15 and 16 January, his effects at Ipswich were sold and his wife and family left the place, having no known residence in this country. He had not the least doubt that if he did not go abroad, he had at least stayed abroad to delay his creditors, which was an act of bankruptcy.

The vice chancellor's decision was that John's petition against a bankruptcy order should be dismissed and he ordered that Halliday's costs in the present case should be taken out of Acton's estate. Because the business partnership had never been officially dissolved, this led to further complications over the claims of Halliday and Mrs Studd to the joint property. However, after the judgement, things moved quite quickly and on 5 May 1828, the stock of the late firm of Studd, Halliday & Acton was advertised for sale. Apart from all the wines, spirits and beer, this included a quantity of coal and a bag of hops. Also included were all the brewing equipment, the two dray horses and the carts used to deliver the barrels of beer to the various public houses belonging to the brewery. Just how many of these the brewery owned was revealed in the advertisement that appeared on 24 May. In Ipswich were The Golden Lion, The King's Head, The Black Horse with its large garden, the premises formerly known as The New Blue Posts in Woodbridge Road with an adjoining dwelling house, plus a small share in The Great White Horse (later to achieve notoriety in Dickens' *Pickwick Papers*). In Harwich the firm owned The Swan and The Golden Lion. In 1826 they had advertised the lease of The New Wherry Inn on the Common Quay at Ipswich but it must have been sold rather than let since it was not included in the current sale. The brewery buildings and the wharf were also to be sold, as were another dwelling house, the Maltings and a wine vault in nearby Foundation Street.

So came to an end a business partnership that had lasted less than fifteen years. Yet John Acton had managed it successfully for at least a dozen years before that for Robert Trotman. Was it that when he became a partner he could not resist taking chances to make money and in so doing lost practically everything? From our point of view the only positive thing to emerge from all that happened is that we now have definite evidence that Eliza was in Paris in December 1826 and that she was said to be ill. Had she, or indeed any of the family, any idea of what was going on? Did the older children who had moved away from the family home have the opportunity to salvage some precious possessions? Indeed, did Mrs Acton and the younger ones accompany John to Calais? Edward, we know, was about to go to London to complete his medical training at the beginning of 1827. Anna, who had been in partnership with Eliza in the school in Woodbridge, was by then a governess in the Norfolk town of Fakenham, where, in 1828, when all the news about her father had become common knowledge in Suffolk, she was quietly married by special licence to John Paul Potter, the surgeon in the Suffolk village of Grundisburgh. Mary, too, had become a governess in Fakenham and the year after her sister she had also married. Her wedding took place at St Marylebone in London; her husband, who was considerably older than her, had lost his first wife the previous year. Anthony Gwynn of Fakenham was a gentleman of substantial means and standing in Norfolk and was very possibly Mary's former employer. With his first wife he had had a family of five daughters and two sons; his eldest daughter had married in 1827, which means that Mary was not much older than some of her stepchildren. She went on to have six children of her own and led a somewhat peripatetic life, for the Gwynns were to be found at different times in Grundisburgh, France, the Channel Islands and Reading. Following her husband's death, Mary returned in the 1870s to live in Ipswich, the only member of the family to retain a connection with the town. On the other hand, Anna's marriage was very short lived; tragically, within a year, at the age of 32, John Potter died in April 1829. It was perhaps fortuitous that Anna was able to offer his medical practice to her brother Edward, who was then in a position to marry Sophia, a vicar's daughter, in 1831. Anna then returned to her former life as a governess, positions also occupied by her sisters Catherine and Susannah.

It is not clear if Mrs Acton had accompanied her husband to France at the beginning of 1827. If she did, then the eminently practical woman that she was, she would soon have been forced to consider what was to be the future of Edgar and John, both of whom were still receiving education. Fortunately, Mrs Acton had family and friends in Kent and it was to them she turned; within months of leaving Ipswich she had settled in the small but fashionable town of Tonbridge, where she rented a house that had previously been used as an academy called Elmden House, but was renamed Bordyke House when she took up the tenancy.

Bordyke House was one of three houses that had been carved out of the original Bordyke Mansion. The records for Tonbridge School show that 14-year-old Edgar was entered as a pupil in 1827. *Pigot's Directory*, that most useful of tools for researchers, reveals that by 1840 Mrs Acton was well established in the town. Heading the alphabetical list of Gentry & Clergy is *Acton, Mrs Eliz, Bordyke House*, while further on in the list, under Lodging House Keepers, we find *Acton, Elizabeth, (& boarding), Bordyke*. It is the word 'boarding' that has led to a possible misunderstanding as to Mrs

Bordyke House, Tonbridge, Kent. (Courtesy of Mr & Mrs A. Miller)

Acton's role. It has been generally held that she ran what amounted to the boarding house of Tonbridge School. At that period many of the pupils were likely to have been day-boys, but in any case, those who did board would have lived in the homes of the headmaster and his assistant where the fees for boarding would have been a most useful addition to their small teaching salaries. The 1841 census may well have contributed to the later confusion by using the term Bordyke for two quite separate establishments. The occupants of the first were the schoolmaster Robert Monk, his wife and their seven children, and six male pupils ranging in age from 10 to 18, the youngest being William de Ramies who had been born in the West Indies and was probably the son of a plantation owner there. Mrs Acton and her family had lived next door. However, it is possible that she may have boarded her daughter Mary's youngest stepson, Hammond Gwynn, who became a pupil of Tonbridge School between the years 1830–6. Part of the misconception that Bordyke House was the school boarding house arose because several of the recipes in *Modern Cookery* bore names connected to the school, such as *Monitors' Tart* and *Tourte à la Judd*, which recalls a major benefactor of the school. No doubt young Edgar and Hammond often filled the house with their hungry school friends and their nicknames for the treats served, stuck.

What we can be fairly sure of is that Mrs Acton, when making her new start, decided that the only way she could keep the family in the manner to which they were accustomed was by making the house work for her, hence her taking such a large house. In a sale notice of 1843 it was described as:

> a substantial brick-built Family residence with desirable frontage of upwards of 110 feet, comprising 3 attics and a lumber room; a good drawing room and best bedroom in front, with 3 bedchambers and 2 servants rooms at rear; Entrance Hall, excellent Dining Room, large Breakfast Parlour and lofty kitchen. Outside a large Brew House and Wash House, Coach House with two-stalled stable and loft over. Carriage entrance.

It all sounds very imposing, which is exactly what Mrs Acton wanted if she was to let lodgings to high-class visitors. At that time, ladies and gentlemen perhaps visiting to take the waters at nearby Tunbridge Wells might hire a suite of rooms – bedroom and sitting room with perhaps a room for a maid who would use the house kitchen to prepare their meals. The layout of the house allowed flexibility for this type of lodging, which could happily bring in several guineas a week. Alternatively, some visitors preferred to have all their meals prepared for them by the house cook and served either in their rooms or in the dining room – at the board (table) – thus becoming 'boarders'. It was perhaps with these boarders that Eliza's interest in cookery grew and the development of new recipes was first tried out when she returned from France to join her mother and younger siblings. If we question why Eliza did not return to teaching either in a school or as a resident governess as her sisters had, the most likely answer is that her recent ill health, or maybe the lack of confidence in herself following her failed love affair, was such that she felt unable to undertake regular employment. There would have been ample opportunities for her to teach in one of the many schools or academies in Tonbridge; one indeed was kept by a Fanny Mercer, who was related to Mrs Acton. Given the fact that Bordyke House had previously been a school, it seems surprising that Eliza did not take the option to return to teaching. The answer to that would seem to point to Mrs Acton having already established her boarding house as a paying concern before Eliza returned from France.

Settling into a town that was half the size of Ipswich and very different in character, closer now to her Aunt Charlotte in East Farleigh as well as all the other Mercer relations, Eliza found a whole new set of acquaintances. She still regarded herself as a poet and was regularly contributing to literary magazines. Some of her work may have been published anonymously, like, as has been suggested, 'The Two Portraits' which appeared in 1835 in the *Sudbury Pocket Book*. Started in 1825 in the Suffolk town of Sudbury and continued successfully for a number of years, the *Pocket Book*, which as

Tonbridge High Street. (From the collection of Tonbridge Historical Society)

its name implies was of a size to fit in a lady's pocket, at that time still a separate entity from a garment, was similar to the modern specialist diary that contains a variety of information. In the case of the Sudbury book its main content was poetry interspersed with engravings of country houses and charming views. In 1831 a collection of the poems appeared in one volume under the title *Poems from Fulcher's Ladies' Memorandum Book and Poetical Miscellany*. In response to the many requests by his readers, ten years later in May 1841, the publisher brought together a revised collection of all the verses that had appeared over the previous seventeen years. George Williams Fulcher was not merely the publisher of other people's work; he used the *Pocket Book* as a vehicle for his own work, modestly signing his poems G.W.F. Others were also designated initials – F.S.M. and Z.Z. – while Mrs or Miss Clara hid her identity with the simple L.B. after her Christian name. Along with Bernard Barton, the Suffolk Quaker poet, and Mrs Hemans, there were two names that were to become important in Eliza's life: Mary and William Howitt. It is likely that Eliza, having read and admired their work, wrote to them and began a friendship that was to last for the rest of her life. Eliza's putative 'The Two Portraits' did not appear in the collected volume, but the Table of Contents does list a poem titled 'The Two Pictures', which was ascribed to a regular contributor who used the nom de plume 'Author of Historical Reveries'. I suggest that this has been mistakenly attributed to Eliza since her verse 'Song', with the name 'Miss Acton' beside it, appears immediately below 'The Two Pictures'.

Five of Eliza's poems were included in the volume. Mr Fulcher claimed that most of the poems in the collection had been written specifically for the *Sudbury Pocket Book*, and certainly none of the five had appeared in her book of 1826. Unfortunately, I have not seen actual copies so can only use their titles to guess at the subject matter, which seems very varied. We are offered 'Song', 'The Violet', 'Song of the Dying', 'To C ******' and 'Stanzas to Helen'. The use of asterisks to disguise identity is a frustratingly annoying habit left over from eighteenth-century newspapers which got round the laws of libel by printing the names of those involved in scandalous affairs in this way. It is likely that the lines dedicated to Helen are for her younger sister.

It is difficult to know if Eliza was accepted by the townspeople of Tonbridge as a poet. To those in the area who had subscribed to her *Poems* she may have been held in high regard, and it would be good to think that her reputation was such that it was the local people who asked her to write and present the 'Ode of Welcome' on their behalf to the dowager Queen Adelaide during the royal visit in 1837. The recently widowed lady was on her way elsewhere when she stopped in the town. This event, although very important to the inhabitants, was not sufficiently so for it to have been remarked on in the local press; neither has Eliza's tribute to the queen-wife who had so lovingly nursed the ailing king-husband been preserved.

In 1832 Edgar left Tonbridge School. Having worked hard at his studies, in his final year, no doubt to his mother's great delight, he had not only won a place at St John's College, Oxford, he had also become a Smythe Exhibitioner, which entitled him to a monetary award to help him through his college days. His matriculation on becoming a member of the college was recorded in the Oxford Alumni for March 1832, but it would appear that when he left the college three years later in 1835 he was not awarded a degree. One cannot help surmising, perhaps wrongly, that once he was away from his mother's influence, he ceased to take his studies seriously. All that is known of his later life is that he went out to Mauritius where he remained for the rest of his days. Nothing has been discovered about his life there, but since there was a strong brewing industry on the island, it may be that Edgar followed his father's profession – or perhaps not, as we shall see later.

And where was John Acton senior all this time? It does not look as if he ever appeared in Tonbridge, and certainly those who later recorded Mrs Acton's time in the town believed her to be a widow. The Oxford reference previously mentioned lists Edgar as being the son of John Acton, Gent, of Ipswich. Yet he certainly had not returned there. Was he still in Calais? A point worth considering is that Tonbridge is much closer to Dover than Ipswich would have been, and it would have been easy for Mrs Acton to make the crossing to France on regular visits to her husband. I have been unable to untangle the complications of the bankruptcy order against him to discover how long it remained in force. His erstwhile partner Halliday had died not long after the bankruptcy file was put in place, so that would have left his executors to pursue matters for his estate and Mary Studd's claim.

All historical and genealogical researchers will know what a defining moment it was when the 1841 census was published. Yet we must treat this important record with caution for things are not always as they seem. Quite apart from the inadvertent mistakes made by the census enumerators, their often-illegible handwriting and those informants who gave incorrect information as to their place of birth and age, the 1841 information is sparse. For example, it was not always clear whether a person not related to the head of the household was a long-term visitor, a lodger, or simply an overnight guest who happened to be present on census day. Much has been made in the past of the fact that when the 1841 census was taken in Tonbridge, Eliza was living alone in Bordyke with only her servant Ann Kirby, a local woman aged 30. Earlier biographers have taken this to mean that Mrs Acton had died. But search the census for the Suffolk village of Grundisburgh, where Edward Acton, the surgeon, was living with his growing family and in the household of farm bailiff James Smith, you will find John and Elizabeth Acton. What we do not know is if they had been there for any length of time or had simply been visiting Edward and were lodged in the house. And in another home, that of the local schoolmaster Edward Robinson, we find not only his wife and two daughters, but also three boy pupils and Helen Acton, described as being of independent means, so not an assistant teacher. It is interesting that when Helen was married by special licence at St George's, Hanover Square, in London, in October of that year, she gave her place of residence as Grundisburgh and her father as John Acton, Esq. The witnesses to the marriage were Anna Potter and Elizabeth Acton, presumably her mother. That her father did not act as a witness suggests he may already have been suffering from ill health. The other witness, M. Fraville, we suppose to have been a French friend of the bridegroom, Nathaniel Ogle, who was assigned the title of 'gent' on the marriage certificate.

Of the other sisters, Anna (Potter) was living as governess to the family of Mr and Mrs Frederick Corrance at Loudham Hall at Pettistree in Suffolk. In contrast, the younger Susannah was part of the very busy and lively household of the surgeon Frederick Fitch and his family at Sible Hedingham in the adjoining county of Essex. Mary, now Mrs Anthony Gwynn, was living at the Chateau Grouaison near Tours in France, from where she would travel to Paris to attend the wedding at the British Embassy of her stepdaughter Emily to George Watson of Fakenham. Catherine Acton was apparently not recorded in any of the census records. That she was still living is borne out by her appearance in later documents, so it is possible that she was abroad at the time. And while Mrs Acton may have waved goodbye to Edgar as he set sail for Mauritius, it must have been much harder for her to lose her youngest son, John, who died at the age of 21.

John was buried in the churchyard of St George the Martyr in London on 18 December 1836. The cause of his death is unknown but as there were a number of burials in the days leading up to his, and five funerals actually on the same day, it is more than likely that there was an epidemic of some kind; outbreaks of influenza, typhoid and cholera were all rife in London between 1836 and 1842. Ironically, his place of death was recorded as being in Suffolk Street. Beyond the dates of his birth and death, we know almost nothing about John. He did not attend Tonbridge School as his brother Edgar did and we have no factual evidence as to why he was living in Southwark. However, we do know that the Royal South London Dispensary where Edward Acton finished his medical training was in Southwark on a site opposite the present Imperial War Museum, and Suffolk Street is less than a mile away from the Dispensary. Thus it is more than likely that John was aiming to follow in his brother Edward's footsteps; possibly the brothers may have planned to go into partnership when John was qualified, and like Edward he was studying for his final diploma when he was taken ill. Possibly he had caught whatever it was from the patients he was treating. If he was studying medicine then that explains why he did not attend Tonbridge School; he would instead have been an apprenticed pupil to a surgeon, as Edward had been to Carew King in Saxmundham.

The church of St George the Martyr where John was buried has an interesting historical context in that one of the walls of the churchyard formed part of the Marshalsea prison, immortalised for posterity by Charles Dickens in *Little Dorrit*. It is not known if John's body was later exhumed, to be reinterred alongside those of his parents, as he is also commemorated at their raised tomb in the graveyard of All Saints, Hastings. If he was, there is no record of which members of the family paid for that to take place and who paid for the rather imposing railed memorial. Like so much else in the lives of the Acton family, questions abound and we have to wait for the answers, in some cases until the next census was taken in 1851, by which time situations would have changed yet again.

FIVE

THE SECOND CAREER

liza is next mentioned in a document dating from 1843. Following the death of her landlord, Francis Woodgate, much of his estate, including Bordyke House, was offered for sale by auction. The notes accompanying the property details describe the house as being rented to Miss Acton, at £50 per annum. That Eliza is now the official tenant must point to the fact that her mother had indeed left Tonbridge for good. That there were no other people registered as being in the house on the night of the 1841 census, apart from her servant Ann Kirby, does not necessarily mean that the house had ceased to offer lodgings. Indeed, with such a high rent, it may have been essential for Eliza to have guests to share her costs. And, it would be pleasant to think that some of these may have assisted her in her new career, which by 1843 was within two years of establishing her once again in the public eye.

It is another of those legends about her that sometime around 1835, possibly just after Fulcher had produced his poetry collection, Eliza made an appointment to see Mr Longman, the publisher, at his office in London. The apocryphal story relates that when she turned up with a folio of poems which she thought he might publish, he waved her proposal aside with the words: 'Don't bring me poems, madam, bring me a cookery book!' No one knows if this is what actually occurred, but Longman was responding, as publishers have always done, to what was considered to be the contemporary taste of the public. Poetry was no longer as fashionable as it had been, especially as it tended to have a limited market. With growing literacy among even the working class, the demand now was for novels, whether they were romances, adventures or those, especially for the young, that imparted a strong moral message. And there were a great many ladies who were only too ready to write such work in return, not as previously for the pleasure of seeing their work in print, but as a way of making a living to support themselves or their families. The question we have to ask is, if this was the trend, then why, knowing that Eliza could write well and from her poems had shown that she was just as capable of transmitting her emotions into novels as the Brontë sisters had, did he challenge her to write a cookery book?

Part of the answer to that may be that Longman had more than enough writers capable of producing novels, but he did not have anyone who could fulfil his desire to capture a market that at the time was dominated by his publishing rival, John Murray. The other contributing factor was that the rapid growth of the middle classes and their spending power had led to the increase of shops selling foodstuffs in far greater quantities than ever before. The export of exotic fruit and vegetables, along with spices and preserves from different parts of the Empire, had filled British grocery stores with unfamiliar foods. Guidance, therefore, was needed to deal with all this bounty that was on offer. In the past, most books dealing with culinary matters had been produced by chefs, usually foreign, who supervised the kitchens in aristocratic and wealthy households where entertaining was done on a large and lavish scale; this bore no resemblance whatsoever to the food eaten by those who did not live in grand country estates with acres of kitchen gardens and glasshouses or large London mansions. However, towards the end of the eighteenth century, there had been a move among the minor gentry, as well as those who had made their money in trade and commerce and were climbing the social ladder, to entertain their guests to well-prepared meals, though on a much smaller scale. To achieve this, the lady of the house needed not just a housekeeper but also a trained cook, who was both able and willing to move with the fashions of the time.

We need to turn to the pages of contemporary literature for clues about the eating habits of the day, and where better to start than with Jane Austen. First we have to understand that meals were taken at times which may seem strange to us. The working man and woman would rise early and begin work on an empty stomach; it might be three hours or more before the fast was broken, offering a short rest to eat a simple meal of perhaps no more than a slice or two of bread. But the working man and woman's diet was such that they would not be in need of a cookery book to tell them how to boil a pudding or make a batch of bread, so the remarks which follow refer to the various tiers of what we call the middle classes; in other words, the type of people who inhabit the pages of the novels of Jane Austen, Mrs Gaskell, Anthony Trollope or Charles Dickens. For them, according to Lydia Bennett in *Pride and Prejudice*, 'breakfast was at ten as usual' – she had then gone on to get married at eleven, so obviously for a young woman this was not necessarily a big meal. Trollope mentions rolls, toast and boiled eggs with perhaps a cold chicken leg accompanied by tea or coffee. Hot chocolate was also on offer in some households and in grander houses there was likely to be a selection of hot meat dishes. Many a school child has been horrified to discover that David Copperfield was served chops for his breakfast at an inn, until they are reminded that he had not just risen from his bed but had been up for some hours and travelled many miles.

The first meal of the day was usually eaten in what became known as the breakfast parlour. This was a smaller room than the formal dining room, and once the cloth was removed the ladies of the house would settle at the table to tend to their work which might include sewing, knitting, painting and drawing or reading. At noon they would go to their rooms to change out of their morning gowns and prepare themselves for afternoon visits. Mrs Gaskell's *Cranford* is excellent for describing the etiquette that surrounded this ritual, which was never supposed to extend beyond a quarter of an hour, thus preventing any serious conversation ever taking place. In some households a light luncheon had been introduced, but the main meal of the day was dinner, usually served around five o'clock. Mutton, veal and venison, as well as beef and pork, were among the favoured meats served, but often there were other courses that included fish and poultry. In *Emma*, which mentions food more than any other Austen novel, we learn that when the Coles, who had made their money in property dealing and were endeavouring to rise in society, gave a dinner party, every corner of the table was covered with a dish. There is a delightful moment in Chapter 10 when the heroine overhears Mr Elton describe a dinner he had attended at the Coles': '... she came in for the Stilton, the North Wiltshire [cheese], the butter, the celery, the beetroot and all the dessert.' It is interesting to note that the influence of the Continent was still very strong with the serving of cheese before the dessert, which would often include a variety of fresh fruit piled high on glass or silver serving dishes, a sure sign of affluence, especially if it was known to come from one's own hothouses.

Following this meal, it was customary for the ladies to withdraw to the drawing room while the gentlemen continued to drink their wine. It was also quite normal to invite other guests to join the party *after* the meal to take tea. This was almost a ritual, the bringing in of the tea tray with its silver urn or kettle on a spirit stove for the ceremonial mixing of the expensive tea, something that could not be entrusted to the domestic staff. Guests then either played cards, listened to music or, if there were sufficient numbers of young people, danced to while away the hours until it was time to leave. Just in case guests might still be hungry, and for those who had come just for the evening, a light supper would be served. When it came to light suppers, there was no one who knew more on that subject than Mr Woodhouse, Emma's father. A gentleman blessed himself with a delicate digestion, he was convinced that suppers were unwholesome. So when he was duty-bound to offer refreshments, his major concern was that his lady guests should eschew the scalloped oysters and minced chicken and have only the plainest of delicacies. He recommended that they join him in a small basin of gruel, but if not that then perhaps a boiled egg, a very small egg, but one that had been prepared as only his housekeeper knew how – that would be wholesome.

'Miss Bates, let Emma help you to a *little* bit of tart – a *very* little bit. Ours are all apple-tarts. You need not be afraid of <u>unwholesome preserves here</u>. [Eliza was to pick up on this subject later in her cookery book.] I do not advise the custard.'

Emma, of course, made sure that the ladies were served with whatever they wished! But throughout the book Mr Woodhouse has much to say on the state of food. When he sent a hindquarter of pork to Miss Bates, it came with instructions on how she should cook it. The leg was to be 'salted but not over-salted and it should be served with boiled turnip, carrot or parsnip. The loin being small and delicate should be made into steaks and fried without grease', since roasting was not good for the stomach. Poor Mr

Woodhouse would have been saddened had he visited the older Musgroves in *Persuasion* and seen the trestles with 'trays bending under the weight of brawn and cold pies'. All in all, Jane Austen provides us with details of party food and picnics – cold lamb and pigeon pies; occasional refreshments which feature cakes and fruit, cold ham and chicken; ices bought from a pastry-cook's shop and French bread for breakfast at *Northanger Abbey*.

Tempting the appetite has, it seems, always been a cure for disappointment in love, but would the modern woman be satisfied with sweetmeats, olives, wine and cherries and a good fire as recommended in *Sense and Sensibility*? The novelist also provides information on the shortage of certain foods such as veal and fish, or the problem of not having a butcher close at hand. And we learn of life before both refrigeration and supermarkets. When Mrs Grant in *Mansfield Park* was given a turkey, she had to cook and eat it midweek because it would not keep until Sunday.

Finally, we need to consider cutlery. The blades of knives were made of steel – not the stainless variety with which we are familiar, but steel which required special cleaning to prevent it rusting and also needed sharpening. For everyday use the handles of both knives and forks were made from horn, the silver cutlery, if one was fortunate enough to have it, being reserved for important occasions. It was forks, however, which were to cause a problem for two of the ladies in Mrs Gaskell's novel, *Cranford*.

Eliza would most certainly have read Jane Austen's novels and it is delightful to think that they may have given her both amusement and some inspiration when she came to undertake her work. *Cranford*, on the other hand, was published after she had begun writing her cookery book. However, this particular episode is worth quoting as it reflects a period Eliza knew well. Miss Matty, Miss Pole and the young narrator were invited to spend the day with Mr Holbrook, who many years before had proposed marriage to Miss Matty. He now lived alone with a housekeeper to take care of all household matters. At the appointed time they sat down to eat:

> We had pudding before meat; and I thought Mr Holbrook was going to make some apology for his old-fashioned ways, for he began: 'I don't know whether you like new-fangled ways.'
>
> 'Oh, not at all!' said Miss Matty.
>
> 'No more do I,' he said. 'My housekeeper will have these in her fashion; or

else I tell her that, when I was a young man, we used to keep strictly to my father's rule: No broth, no ball; no ball, no beef; and always began dinner with broth. Then we had suet puddings, boiled in the broth with the beef; and then the meat itself. If we did not sup our broth, we had no ball, which we liked better; and the beef came last of all, and only those had it who had done justice to the broth and the ball. Now folks begin with sweet things, and turn their dinners topsy-turvy.'

After this homily and the pudding, came not beef but ducks and green peas. Instead of being delighted, the ladies looked at their plates in consternation:

We had only two-pronged black-handled forks [similar to a modern short-handled carving-fork]. It is true the steel was as bright as silver; but what were we to do? Miss Matty picked up her peas, one by one, on the point of the prongs ... Miss Pole sighed over her delicate young peas as she left them on one side of her plate untasted, for they *would* drop between the prongs. I looked at my host; the peas were going wholesale into his capacious mouth, shovelled up by his large, round-ended knife. I saw, I imitated, I survived!

By the time Eliza came to write her book fashions had changed. In her instructions for what she called *The Young Wife's Pudding*, she begins: 'Break separately into a cup four perfectly sweet eggs, and with the point of a small three-pronged fork clear them from the specks.'

Instruction manuals on housekeeping in general and cooking in particular had been in existence for years. Long before the days of printing, handwritten copies of the meals served by the chefs of kings and noblemen had been passed down through the generations. But the eighteenth century brought a demand from a wider market. Eliza must have studied the works of her immediate predecessors. Of these the first was Hannah Glasse (1708–70), whose *The Art of Cookery Made Plain and Easy* was published in 1747, almost 100 years before Eliza's work. The first edition of *The Art of Cookery* did not bear Mrs Glasse's name but was ascribed as being 'by a Lady' and 'printed for the Author and sold at Mrs Ashburn's China shop at the corner of Fleet Ditch'. Initially, the public found it hard to believe that the book had been written by a woman, it being rumoured that the author was a Dr Hill. The book proved immensely popular and in the posthumous edition of 1784, twenty-six publishers, including Thomas Longman, had a share in its production. Mrs Glasse, we are told, did all the cooking herself and included many useful chapters, including one on preserving food for the benefit of captains of ships. The last edition of her book was printed in 1824.

Next came *The Experienced English Housekeeper*, for the use and ease of ladies, housekeepers and cooks etc., by Elizabeth Raffald (1733–81). This was another work based on years of practice. Before her marriage, Elizabeth had spent fifteen years in service as a housekeeper, her last employment being with the Warburtons of Arley Hall in Cheshire. At the age of 30 she had married John Raffald and moved to Manchester where her husband was a gardener and florist. During the next eighteen years she gave birth to fifteen daughters! Yet she still found time to open a shop which sold prepared meats such as ham and tongue, pickles and soups, but also served as a recruitment agency for domestic staff. In 1766 she was making and selling bridal and christening cakes, and three years later she produced a book containing 800 original recipes. The first edition was financed by subscribers who paid 5s for their copies, while those on general sale cost 6s. The cult of celebrity and the importance of publicity were not unknown in the eighteenth century, Mrs Raffald charging 7s for a signed copy. Her next venture was to open a cooking school in Manchester and finally she became the licensee of the King's Head in Salford. After her death at the age of only 47, her influence continued with the publication of thirteen genuine editions of her book and twenty-three pirated ones. The last edition appeared in 1806.

An altogether different production was *A New System of Domestic Cookery* by 'a Lady', which appeared in 1805. Hiding behind the anonymity of 'a Lady' was the mature figure of Mrs Maria Rundell who was born in 1745. On her marriage to the surgeon Thomas Rundell, they lived in Bath where she brought up her family of three daughters and two sons and where, as a young bride and later mother, she had to find out the hard way all that was involved in running a household. Following her husband's death in 1800, she often went to stay with her married daughters as well as friends; in particular she was drawn to the London home of her brother-in-law Phillip Rundell, a goldsmith in Ludgate Hill, who also employed one of her sons. Throughout her marriage Maria made copious notes about all kinds of domestic matters and copied out the receipts for dishes produced in her kitchen, as well as the menus for dinner parties she had given. It was while she was sorting out all her papers that she conceived the idea of putting all this valuable information into book form for the benefit of her daughters. Phillip Rundell numbered among his old friends and acquaintances John Murray, the publisher in nearby Fleet Street. By 1803, John Murray junior, then aged 25, had taken over the business and like most young men he was eager to develop it and take it into new fields. Whether it was a casual conversation between Maria and Murray at a social gathering, or a more formal approach to him for advice on how to deal with her collection of wisdom, is unimportant; the main thing is that in November 1805 eleven copies of the book were printed and entered in the Stationer's Register.

Murray, believing he was on to a winner, offered the work to booksellers on subscription. Three hundred advance copies were ordered and the initial print run, thought to be several thousand, sold out in six months. No fee changed hands; Murray had not offered one and Maria had not expected it. However, the book was a tremendous success, and in 1808 Murray gave Maria a cheque for £150 for 'her gift to me of *Domestic Cookery*', in other words the copyright. In the years that followed the book continued to sell like the proverbial hot cakes, between 5,000 and 10,000 copies annually. It is possible that Maria's family and friends thought she should have received much more than £150 and the occasional parcel of newly published books from Murray's. So it was that towards the end of 1819, Maria approached Longmans hoping they might regain the copyright for her and bring out any future editions of *Domestic Cookery*. A legal battle ensued between the two publishers that rumbled on for several years. Maria eventually received a settlement of 2,000 guineas by instalments from Murray, but Longmans had lost out on what promised to be a continuing money-spinner. Small wonder then that following Maria's death in 1829, Thomas Longman was looking for his own cookery book writer.

According to Eliza, her *Modern Cookery* was ten years in the making. The first advertisement for it appeared in *The Morning Chronicle* on 18 January 1845, so we know she must have started the work around 1834. It was from 1842 onwards that entries concerning 'Acton's Cookery' first appear in Longmans Ledgers. In March 1844 there was an entry for a payment for thirty drawings of cooking utensils to illustrate the book, and that was followed in May by a payment to a Miss Williams for engravings and woodcuts, which suggests that Eliza had already submitted her manuscript by then. It is in the most unlikely places that one finds intriguing details. Following the item of the engravings is another that reads: 'July 16, Websters Eng. Dict. & Books to Miss Acton'. We know that John Murray had been in the habit of presenting new books to Mrs Rundell, so perhaps Longman adopted the same practice – but Webster's Dictionary? Does this mean that Eliza could not spell correctly? That seems unlikely, but it is possible that she was accustomed to the eighteenth-century spelling of words, which had lately been updated, and since the American Webster's was at the time the leading authority, it was only right she should have a copy. The gift raises all manner of questions: was it just a gift? Was Eliza pleased to receive it or slightly annoyed at the possible implication behind it?

Surprisingly, Longman did not go all out to present this new book as being very different from Mrs Rundell's popular work, for the advertisement states that it is: 'Dedicated to the Young Housekeepers of England', just as *Domestic Cookery* had been intended. The blurb told readers that '*Modern Cookery in all its Branches*, was reduced to a system of easy practice for the use of private families. In a series of receipts, all of which have been strictly tested, and are given with the most minute exactness. By Eliza Acton.' No hiding behind a nom de plume for Eliza. It was this *minute exactness* which was to make Eliza's receipts stand out from all those which had preceded it, and so set the tone for all future cookery writers. It was she who, for the first time, gave a brief but exact summary of the ingredients used in a dish. Compare, for example, Mrs Rundell's instructions for Brown Bread Pudding:

> Half a pound of stale brown bread grated, ditto of currants, ditto of shred suet, sugar & nutmeg; mix with four eggs, a spoonful of brandy, and two spoonfuls of cream; boil in a cloth or basin that exactly holds it, three or four hours.

Eliza's receipt takes longer to read but is in well-written prose that makes careful distinctions; for example, bread is to be not just grated, it is to be finely grated and the eggs are to be beaten before being added to the other

Page from Longmans Ledgers. (From the Special Collections, University of Reading) ingredients. In other words, Eliza is living up to her claims that she is writing for the novice as well as the more proficient cook.

> To half a pound of stale brown bread, finely and lightly grated, add an equal weight of suet chopped small, and of currants cleaned and dried, with half a saltspoonful of salt, three ounces of sugar, the third of a small nutmeg grated, two ounces of candied peel, five well-beaten eggs, and a glass of brandy. Mix these ingredients thoroughly, and boil the pudding in a cloth for three hours and a half. Send port wine sauce to table with it. The grated rind of a large lemon may be added to this pudding with good effect.

And then follows her innovation:

> Brown bread, suet and currants, each 8 oz; sugar, 3 oz; candied peel, 2 oz; salt, ½ saltspoonful; ⅓ of small nutmeg; eggs, 5; brandy, 1 wineglassful; 3½ hours.

This careful listing of ingredients has become standard in modern cookery books and woe betide the editor who omits some vital ingredient, which unfortunately happens occasionally to recipes both in books and on the Internet. There is nothing more frustrating for the cook who finds that either the instruction for when to add a certain ingredient is missing or, out of the blue, another ingredient is introduced. Perhaps it was Eliza's early training as a schoolmistress that made her instructions so clear. Mrs Rundell, you will notice, gives no indication of how much nutmeg to use, or what size spoon should be used to measure the brandy and the cream. That little detail of cleaning and drying the currants may not be important today, but it certainly was in the early nineteenth century when dried fruit was imported in sacks that went straight to the shops and from which the desired amounts were measured out for customers. The young wife or housekeeper might have been unaware that bits of grit as well as the fruit stalks could be found among the currants, raisins and sultanas she had purchased. It is comments like that and her observations, such as here that grated lemon rind would add to the flavour of the pudding, that make the reader feel as if she is with you in the kitchen. That she did not take herself so seriously as to become pompous is shown in the following verse, said to have been written to one of her sisters:

If you want a good pudding, to teach you I'm willing:

Take two pennyworth of eggs, when twelve for a shilling,

And of the same fruit, that Eve once had chosen,

Well pared and well chopped, at least half a dozen;

Six ounces of bread – let your maid eat the crust,

The crumbs must be grated as small as dust;

Six ounces of currants from the stones you must sort,

Lest they break out your teeth, and spoil all your sport;

Six ounces of sugar won't make it too sweet,

Some salt and some nutmeg will make it complete;

Three hours let it boil, without hurry or flutter,

And then serve it up, without sugar or butter.

In less than a month after publication, Longman placed an expanded advertisement for the book using reviews from various sources. *The Globe*, for example, said 'her receipts are distinguished for excellence, The dishes prepared according to Miss Acton's directions – all of which, she tells us, have been tested and approved – will give satisfaction by their delicacy, and will be found economical in price as well as delicious in flavour'. *The Weekly Dispatch* called the book 'the most perfect compendium, or rather cyclopaedia, of the art of modern cookery ever yet offered to the public'. Praise indeed, as was *The Atlas*': 'The arrangement adopted by Miss Acton is excellent. She has trusted nothing to others. She has proved all she has written by personal inspection and experiment.' By May there was a new and greatly improved edition about which *The Morning Post* said: 'Miss Acton may congratulate herself on having composed a work of great utility, and one that is finding its way to every "dresser" in the kingdom. Her cookery book is unquestionably the most valuable compendium of the art that has yet been published.' And what did *The Ipswich Journal* have to say about their erstwhile resident who had apparently achieved some fame? Following a critique of M. Thiers' *History of the Consulate and Empire*, came the ponderous:

Having made mention of works calculated to give ample food to the mind, we are now invited to another theme: *Modern Cookery in all its branches* by

Miss Eliza Acton with numerous woodcuts. We are inclined to think that this little work will bear the severest test of practice. The illustrations it gives are calculated to facilitate the labours of cookery, comprising a variety of receipts, with the quantities of the ingredients and the time required to prepare them for the table. Many are suited to the palate of the most luxurious, others to the invalid; forming altogether a useful and practical guide to the housekeeper who has a varied taste to satisfy.

Reviews of the book quickly appeared in newspapers throughout the country. Recognising the fact that Eliza's work was somewhat different to that of other cookery books, with 'directions ... so practical, clear and simple', as early as 13 February 1845 the reviewer for *The Aberdeen Journal* continued:

Many books on cookery are liable to this objection, that they contain receipts purely theoretical, & which the authors have never themselves reduced to practice ... Miss Acton gives directions entirely new. The work is profoundly illustrated by neat woodcuts; and we predict will soon be found in all the kitchens of any pretence in the country.

All these remarks must have gladdened Eliza's heart, though one wonders what she made of the review in *The Newcastle Courant*. Plainly the critic was not happy that he had been asked to make a judgement on a cookery book.

The precise merits of this bulky volume do not come within the ordinary canon of criticism. All that can be said of it by those not actually professional cooks amounts to this, that the receipts are explained with praiseworthy minuteness, that they are arranged with analytical skill & that they are so numerous as to fill nearly 700 pages. With these varied recommendations Acton's 'Cookery' ought to be a sine qua non in the economy of every household.

In all probability Eliza would have smiled at the reluctance of the curmudgeonly critic to admit that her book was good. Her ten years' labour had paid off, quite literally, when six months after publication she received in June from Longmans the sum of £67 11s 2d, her share of the profits on the sales. However, she was not given long to sit back and enjoy her success because with each new edition there were new receipts to add, as well as printing errors to correct. Furthermore, there was a new project to be undertaken, for as she had been working on *Modern Cookery*, she had realised that there was a very definite demand for a good handbook on Invalid Cookery.

SIX

COMBINING THE INGREDIENTS

M ost of Eliza's immediate predecessors had laid the foundations for their cookery books based on years of experience either as working housekeepers in large, affluent households or, like Mrs Rundell, after a lifetime of running her own home. They had all written down and kept the recipes that had worked for them, whether they were copied directly from someone else or were their own variation of a well-known dish. Only a few years younger than Eliza, the Frenchman Alexis Soyer had garnered some of his experience as a practising chef in restaurants in Paris. In 1826 he was the chief cook at one of the fashionable cafés in the Boulevard des Italiens. If only it was possible to prove that in that same year, when we know Eliza was in Paris, she had dined at the restaurant and had been influenced by Soyer's mode of cooking. Certainly they were later to share many ideas about nutrition and the general health of the population, as well as practising a sensible, economical approach to the buying of food and its preparation. It is very likely that once Soyer had fled to England after the second French Revolution of 1830, and become chef of the Reform Club in London, their paths crossed again.

It is also likely that Eliza honed her own cooking skills while she was in France, where she must have been made aware of the general European opinion that British cooking was inferior to that of other countries. She felt very strongly that this should not be so, especially as Britain was so rich in the abundant and varied produce of its own agriculture and that imported from its colonies. She put much of the blame for this ill opinion on 'our own strong and stubborn prejudice against innovation in general and the innovations of strangers in particular'. Fortunately, she remarked, the nation had in recent times become more liberal in its attitudes and was prepared to experiment with food, just as in the second half of the twentieth century the increase in foreign holidays and the migration from the Caribbean and the Indian subcontinent changed our eating habits. In France, one imagines, she had learned to appreciate the everyday family cookery as well as that of the café. Thus she would have carried back home with her the instructions for making her favourite dishes. These may have provided the beginnings of her collection, but how was she to find enough recipes to fill a book such as Longmans required?

She began by researching the market and reading all the books on cookery and household management that were available at the time. From these she was able to decide how to shape her own book. Excellent though most of them were, they did not fulfil what she considered was the most important criterion, namely the provision of easily understood and helpful instruction for the totally inexperienced housekeeper. Here she was thinking of the young, newly married woman, now mistress of a household, who, having not had the opportunity of acquiring such knowledge at home, finds that her ignorance of domestic economy leaves her unable to conduct her household concerns as she would wish. In the preface to the first edition of *Modern Cookery in All its Branches*, with her hypothetical bride in mind, Eliza reveals her motivation and what it is that makes her book unique:

> Thrown thus entirely upon her own resources, she [the young mistress] will naturally and gladly avail herself of the aid to be derived from such books as can really afford her the information she requires. Many admirably calculated to do this, are already in the possession of the public; but amongst the larger number of works on cookery, which we have carefully perused, we have never yet met with one which appeared to us either quite intended for, or entirely suited to the need of the totally inexperienced; none in fact, which contained the first rudiments of the art, with directions so practical, clear and simple, as to be understood and easily followed, by those who had no previous knowledge of the subject.

This surely is Eliza the good teacher, showing how in the past she had set about educating her pupils.

In discussing household servants, it becomes clear that Eliza had a very strong, perhaps even radical, opinion about their qualifications for the posts they held. Her words may strike a chord with modern readers. Talking about the girls who were employed as cooks in middle-class homes, she writes:

> It can scarcely be expected that good cooks should abound amongst us, if we consider how very few receive any training to fit them for their business. Every craft has its apprentices;[15] but servants are generally left to scramble together as they can, from any source which accident may open to them a knowledge of their respective duties. We have often thought, that schools in which these duties should be taught them thoroughly, would be of far greater benefit to them than is the half knowledge of comparative un-useful matters so frequently bestowed on them by charitable educationists.

There is no better example in literature of the point Eliza is making than the Price household in *Mansfield Park*. Mrs Price was one of those pretty, flighty young women, brought up with absolutely no knowledge of domestic affairs, expecting to marry a wealthy husband as her sister Lady Bertram had done. However, her choice of an impecunious husband and the consequent large family had left her at the mercy of maids such as those described by Eliza. They were cheap and truculent, and having had no leadership from Mrs Price did only want they wanted, the cook girl producing food which Fanny Price, on a visit from the home of her wealthy adoptive relations, could only deem as 'unrefined'. Mrs Gaskell in *Cranford* features the 'little charity school maiden' who is Mrs Forester's only servant. This girl, barely in her teens, was so small she needed help to carry the tea trays when her mistress was entertaining. However, there is a difference between this household and that of the Prices'; Mrs Forrester takes the time to teach her maid and one knows that the girl will learn more from her mistress than she ever did from her school.

So Eliza had in mind the servant, too, when she compiled her book, one that was to have 'such thoroughly explicit and minute instruction as may, we trust, be readily comprehended and carried out by <u>any class</u> of

learners, on receipts, moreover, with a few trifling exceptions which are
scrupulously specified, are confined to such as may be *perfectly depended on*
[her italics]'. She then gives some insight into the practicalities involved
in the preparation of the book. She tells us that most of the receipts
have been tested 'beneath our own roof and under our own personal
inspection'. She was, as one of the few letters to her proves, still living
in Bordyke House at this time. We may picture her in the kitchen
accompanied by the trusty Ann Kirby, trying out the receipts she had
collected as well as creating new ones. Were there just the two of them?
Did Ann do most of the actual cooking while Eliza made detailed notes?
Although the 1841 census reveals Ann as the only servant, it is likely
that Eliza had the help of kitchen maids who lived locally. When Eliza uses
the term 'we' in the preface to the book, it may be that she is using the
authorial third person, but it is also possible that she was including her
trusted kitchen assistants in the statement: 'We have trusted nothing to
others, but having desired sincerely to render the work one of genuine
usefulness, we have spared neither cost nor labour to make it so.' To have
been a kitchen maid in Eliza Acton's household would have provided an
education worth its weight in gold, if not literally, then certainly worth a
good salary in any future employment.

From her own experience Eliza knew what it was like to try to maintain
standards on a limited income, so cost was something that concerned her
greatly. She was very conscious that at the time she was writing, during
the latter part of the 1830s and early 1840s, the British economy was
yet again under great pressure. Writing of how grateful a husband must
be when he has a wife who supervises the household expenditure wisely,
she remarks: 'This, at a period when the struggle for income is so general,
and the means of half the families holding a certain rank in the world are
so insufficient for the support of their position, is a consideration of very
deep importance.' Her words certainly ring true as we enter the second
decade of the twenty-first century. Although Eliza was unique at that
time for a woman writing a cookery book, in that she was single and not a
professional, she obviously had a wide and intimate acquaintance among
those who were married, and being, as she had earlier described herself,
'an on-looker', she had no doubt witnessed some of the marital tensions
that arose as a result of poor housekeeping.

Having done her background reading and determined how she wished to present her book, Eliza was then faced with collecting the receipts to fill the pages. Unlike her predecessors with their vast store, she had to expand what she had and find new material from somewhere. But where? The answer is that yet again Eliza was ahead of her time; she adopted a method, much used during recent memory as a means of fundraising, whether for a major charity or the local school, of enlisting the support of celebrities and people of standing in the community, asking them to provide her with details of their favourite dishes. Some of these recipes would have been relayed by word of mouth, particularly from those with whom she was on visiting terms, but she must have written to the other selected contributors. It is a wonder she had time, when the replies came, to test them all. Although we have no knowledge of how she worded her request, each letter must have contained sufficient appeal to satisfy the recipients that it would be to their advantage to have their names appended to a specific dish. Of course, it was tacitly understood that the actual copying out of the receipt would be done by the cook or housekeeper, whoever was responsible for producing the dish.

In many larger households the position of cook-housekeeper had become separated, since the introduction of formal training schools for cooks was producing professionally qualified women whose sole responsibility was to prepare and present good meals. The housekeeper was then left to oversee the smooth running of the rest of the household. For the middle-class family whose income did not stretch to the employment of both cook and housekeeper, the best option was to have a good cook. And it was here that Eliza again came to the fore. She realised that for the good cook to operate well within the household, her mistress must be in a position to supervise what went on in the kitchen; the lady of the house must have a knowledge of the quality of produce used and must be able to trust her cook to buy wisely and well, and not try to siphon off part of her budget into her own purse. In her role as teacher, Eliza has much to say on the duties of the mistress of the house, not only on instructing her daughters how to cook but also on how to train her staff. She has some stern words about households like that of Mrs Price in *Mansfield Park*:

> Few things are more certain to involve persons of narrow fortune in painful difficulties than the ruinous extravagance which so often exists in every

department of a house of which the sole regulation is left to the servants, who, more than any other class of people in the world appear to be ignorant of the true value of money, and of the means of economizing it ... the greatest number are reckless enough in their wasteful profusion when uncontrolled by the eye of a superior.

As well as asking for receipts, Eliza was careful to acknowledge the source of well-known dishes, a habit not generally followed by those who came before or after her. For example, she includes Monsieur Ude's receipt 'Hams superior to Westphalia', adding below the title the word 'Excellent'. Louis Ude had been cook to the French king, Louis XVI, then to the Earl of Sefton, and steward to HRH the Duke of York. His book, *The French Cook. A System Adapted to the Use of English Families*, appeared first in 1813. When she copied out his receipt, Eliza enclosed it within quotation marks to show its provenance. The instructions are for curing the ham, and in her observations Eliza remarks that she is sure that any reader trying this method will find that it really does produce a ham that is superior to Westphalian ham. Perhaps showing loyalty to the county of her childhood, in her own version of the receipt she chooses a leg of Suffolk farmhouse pork to cure. She then reveals that after testing the method for some years with good results, 'we had it adopted for curing bacon too'. This is then followed by a receipt labelled 'Bordyke Receipt', a reference to the house in which she lived in Tonbridge where most of the testing of receipts was carried out. While today's cook is unlikely to actually cure a ham at home – even if one were able to purchase the necessary saltpetre easily, it is possible that one might wish to cook a ready-cured ham for a special occasion. In that case, Eliza offers some useful and interesting tips on how to decorate it. In England, she tells us,

when a ham has been carefully and delicately boiled, the rind while it is still warm, may be carved in various fanciful shapes to decorate it; and a portion of it left round the knuckle in a semicircular form of four or five inches deep, may at all times be easily scollopped [sic] at the edge or cut into points. This, while preserving a character of complete simplicity for the dish, will give it an air of neatness and finish at a slight cost of time and trouble. A paper frill should be placed round the bone.

From her careful research of the subject she has discovered that 'the Germans cut the ham-rind after it has been stripped from the joint, into small leaves and similar "prettinesses", and arrange them in a garland, or other approved device, upon its surface. (*This should be done with a confectionery or paste cutter.)' While 'in Ireland and elsewhere, bread evenly sliced, and stamped out with cutters much smaller than a fourpenny-piece,[16] then carefully fried or coloured in the oven, is used to form designs upon hams after they are glazed'. This is then followed by advice on how to use savoury jelly as a garnish and where to find details of making this plus directions on carving. Can't you just hear Eliza telling her pupils of years gone by: 'If a job's worth doing, it's worth doing well'? And can you not also hear her as a modern television cook giving you not only her clear instructions but also the confidence to try a dish for yourself?

Created for the Russian statesman, Nesselrode Pudding, a confection of chestnuts, egg whites and whipped cream, was both a fashionable and favourite pudding served at the tables of grander houses. Again, Eliza gives credit to the originator, Monsieur Carême, stating that as she has not had the opportunity of making it herself, she gives his own receipt, he being the best authority for it.[17] However, she does suggest various ways of adapting it. She does not state if Nesselrode cream was also Carême's creation, and neither does she identify which countess was the inspiration for Crème à la Comtesse, but possibly her readers would have known that. This was another dish made with Spanish chestnuts, placed in a mould and left in a cool place for six to eight hours at which point it could be decorated.

> It has a pretty appearance when partially stuck with pistachio-nuts, blanched, dried and cut in spikes, their bright green colour rendering them very ornamental to dishes of this kind; as they are, however, much more expensive than almonds, they can be used more sparingly, or intermingled with spikes of the firm outer rind of candied citron.

Citron seems to be one of those things no longer generally available to us. It was similar to a lemon, smaller than we are used to and with a much thicker skin. It was possible years ago to buy it candied for use in cooking, but it seems to have been replaced by the ubiquitous mixed peel of oranges and lemon.

In some respects, Eliza Acton's *Modern Cookery* reads like pages from *Who's Who*. But it is hard to believe she really approached Her Majesty Queen Victoria and Prince Albert for the receipts of their favourite puddings. It is likely these would have appeared in magazines. Eliza commends the Queen's Pudding to her readers, describing it as being extremely delicate, but she cannot resist putting her own stamp on it by suggesting that it be served with a compôte of currants, cherries or plums, and she tweaks it by replacing the vanilla flavouring in the original with bitter almonds, lemon rind, noyau (a liqueur brandy flavoured with fruit kernels), 'or aught else which may be better liked than the vanilla'. The reader who has watched television cookery competitions may be amused to hear Eliza's words of over 150 years ago echoed in the warning: 'The cook must be reminded that unless the eggs be stirred briskly as the boiling milk is gradually poured to them, they will be likely to curdle.'

Another royal contribution, albeit one that did not appear until the 1855 edition, but which showed how up to the minute Eliza was in her editing, came from the household of the King of Oudh. Visiting London in December 1856, Mr and Mrs Herbert Cotton from the Ipswich area attended a performance of *A Midsummer Night's Dream* at the Princess's Theatre.[18] Mrs Cotton later wrote in her diary: 'The King of Oude [sic] and his suite were in the theatre this evening and attracted a great deal of attention. The jewels worn by the King were of enormous size and lustre.' Obviously the opulence of the jewellery was too ostentatious for her taste and when it came to copying out the dish, Eliza may have shared her opinion with regard to some of the ingredients. Labelled as 'An Omlet' (sic), the receipt included cayenne pepper, mint, and leeks or onions. Eliza sensibly adapted the amount of each ingredient, remarking that the original was very fiery and unlikely to find many admirers. If she had a knowledge of the Indian system of weights, she did not see fit to translate them, for the instructions she gave read: 'Five eggs, two tolahs of milk, one masha of salt, two mashas of cayenne pepper, three of mint, and two tolahs of leeks'.

Still in the upper echelons of society, via the Earl of Sefton's erstwhile chef, M. Ude, came what were called ramekins or Sefton Fancies, which sound somewhat similar to cheese straws, only circular, served very hot. The Duke of York's name is appended to a custard, the very ingredients of which make one's mouth water. 'Brandied Morella cherries, ½ to whole pint; boiled custard, (properly made, of course!) from 1 to 1 ½ pints; thick cream, ½ pint or more; brandy, 1 to 2 glassesful; sugar, 2 to 3 oz; juice of ½ large lemon; prepared cochineal, or carmine, 20 to 40 drops.' The dish was assembled by placing the drained cherries thickly at the base of the glass serving dish, covering them with the cold custard and then garnishing the edge with macaroons or Naples biscuits, or piling some firmly whipped rose-coloured cream, highly flavoured with brandy, on the top. This was a dish one can imagine that Emma Woodhouse might well have had served to the lady guests who came to keep her father company.[19]

The artist, Sir Edwin Landseer's Pudding, seems to be very similar to Eliza's original receipt known as The Welcome Guest's Own Pudding, described as light and wholesome. Unfortunately, we do not know the identity of the Good Captain or the Colonel, both of whom provided details of biscuits which, though from a plain, simple mixture of flour and milk or thin cream, Eliza declares to be excellent and wholesome. In contrast to these are Threadneedle Street Biscuits, almost certainly provided by a banker. Appropriately, the quantity produced is large and the biscuits much richer; both butter and sugar being added to the flour before mixing with milk. Eliza admits that she has not tested the result of adding half a teaspoonful of bicarbonate of soda to the mixture, but she does suggest that caraway seeds (much despised by children before the Second World War) can be added, if they are liked! The one biscuit maker we do know something about was Aunt Charlotte, whose receipt follows that of the Colonel's. This was Mrs Charlotte Miller, the widowed, childless aunt of Eliza who lived in Teston, and who played a large part in the lives of all her nieces.

We must remind ourselves that Eliza was writing at a time when the average household was much larger than it is today, hence it may appear from the amount of ingredients used that the dishes are extravagant. And only a very small proportion of her receipts were for rich puddings; she happily provided ideas for the more mundane rice pudding, for example. The same applied to her use of vegetables, surprising us with a number of variations of how to cook the humble potato. In her chapter on vegetables, she prefaces her instructions on the preparation of potatoes by remarking on its nutritional value. Her remarks offer a stark reminder of what life was like for the poorest members of the population. 'It [the potato] *must* be very nutritious, or it would not sustain the strength of thousands of people whose almost sole food it constitutes, and who, when they can procure a sufficient supply of it to satisfy fully the demands of hunger, are capable of accomplishing the heaviest daily labour.' With what can only be a reference to the situation in Ireland, she warns against dependency on one vegetable to provide subsistence. She goes on to say: 'we can easily comprehend the predilection of an entire people for a tuber which combines, like the potato, the solidity almost of bread, with the healthful properties of other various fresh vegetables, without their acidity.'

In a footnote to these remarks, Eliza demonstrates how seriously she took her subject. She has not simply put together a series of interesting receipts; she has studied the whole subject of nutrition. She refers to Dr Jonathan Pereira's 1841 publication, *The Elements of Materia Medica*, which included the scientific observations of Dr Baly on the properties contained within the potato, namely that they could both prevent and cure scurvy. Warming to her subject, Eliza cannot help adding a general reprimand on the poor way that potatoes were cooked in many English households. Not only was all their nutritional value destroyed, but this led to the appalling waste of them when cold, even during the season when the price was highest. One can imagine that when Eliza sat down to check her manuscript before publication, she read through what she had written about wastage and, fired up by the subject, decided to append the following footnote:

> We cannot refrain from a few words of remark here on the daily waste of wholesome food in this country which constitutes one of the most serious domestic abuses that exist amongst us; and one which it is most painful to witness while we see at the same time the half-starvation of large masses of our people. It is an evil which the steady and resolute opposition of the educated classes would soon greatly check, and which ought not vainly to appeal to their good sense and good feeling, augmenting, as it must, the privations of the scantily-fed poor; for the waste of one part of the community cannot fail to increase the 'want' of the remainder.

This was fighting talk indeed. Eliza the social reformer was beginning to show her hand.

She gave fourteen different ways of serving the humble potato, including regional variations from Ireland and Lancashire. One bears the name of Captain Kater, the son of a German-born sugar baker in Bristol. He entered the Army where he became involved in scientific work, eventually achieving some fame as the inventor of the improved Madras pendulum. He married into a fortune and was able to devote himself to scientific work, becoming a fellow of the Royal Society. His method of cooking potatoes is, to say the least, somewhat labour intensive, insofar as when they are cooked and drained, each potato is laid individually on a warm cloth which is then twisted to remove all the moisture from it, at the same time making it perfectly round in shape. Each is then put in a warmed dish and placed before the fire until all are ready to be served. The interesting thing about this method, as far as Eliza was concerned, was that it left the potatoes in an ideal state for use in puddings or cakes where they acted as a substitute for flour.

Other contributions came from those who preferred the anonymity of a pseudonym, such as 'Our Little Lady's Receipt' and 'The Good Daughter's Mincemeat Pudding', which suggests that they were supplied by members of her family. Is it possible to detect a case of sibling rivalry in the naming of the latter? Or was this perhaps an example of Eliza's sense of humour, as is shown in her directions for baking mackerel or whiting, two fish known for being cheap yet very nutritious, which she called Cinderella's Receipt? Another one, she confides to us, had long been passed between the friends and acquaintances of a distinguished, but now deceased poet. She makes a point of saying that she has permission to print it – in other words, she was not trying to pass it off as her own – but the fact that it was written in mock poetic form would have appealed to her greatly.

THE POET'S RECEIPT FOR SALAD

Two large potatoes, passed through kitchen sieve
Unwonted softness to the salad give:
Of mordent mustard, add a single spoon,
Distrust the condiment which bites so soon;
But deem it not, thou man of herbs, a fault,
To add a double quantity of salt;
Three times the spoon with oil of Lucca crown,
And once with vinegar, procured from town;
True flavour needs it, and your poet begs

The pounded yellow of two well-boiled eggs;
Let onion atoms lurk within the bowl,
And scarce suspected, animate the whole;
And lastly, in the flavoured compound toss
A magic teaspoon of anchovy sauce:
Then, though green turtle fail, though venison's tough,
And ham and turkey are not boiled enough,
Serenely full, the epicure may say –
Fate cannot harm me, – I have dined to-day.

As was her custom, Eliza listed all the required amounts of ingredients, adding the injunction to thoroughly stir up (toss) the salad immediately before dinner. This receipt is guaranteed to raise a smile and is certainly worth trying, but please heed Eliza's note: 'As this salad is the result of great experience and reflection, it is hoped young salad-makers will not attempt to make any improvements upon it.' It is the readers' choice to interpret this note as they wish.

Among the many interesting things she has to say in the chapter on eggs is a note on preserving them. Those readers brought up during the Second World War will no doubt remember that their mothers stored precious eggs by placing them in large earthenware bowls filled with isinglass. Eliza's recommendation was to paint each egg very carefully with gum Arabic before storing it. But from a historical point of view, more fascinating is the footnote she gave on the subject of storing eggs at sea: 'An old and experienced cook from on board a man-of-war, directs eggs to be rubbed with salt butter, and packed in layers with plenty of bran between them. He says that the salt penetrates the shell and tends to preserve the eggs, which will require no additional salt when eaten.' She concluded the footnote with the statement: 'we give the information to the reader as we received [it].' Was this second-hand information or did she actually meet the old and experienced sea-cook? I have a mental picture of Eliza, notebook in hand, sitting on an upturned boat on the beach at one of the Kent seaside towns listening to the old seafarer as he imparts his store of knowledge of cooking aboard ship.

It was probably at one of these towns that she came across turkeys' eggs for sale. She tells us she knows that these do not reach the London market in great numbers, but constant supplies were brought over from France to the coastal towns of Kent and Sussex. She describes the eggs as being of large size but nonetheless their flavour was delicate and they could be boiled for the breakfast table or used wherever a hen's egg was required. The advantage the turkey egg had over that of the hen was that the thickness of its shell made it edible for longer; plus, an important consideration, they were reasonable in price. More surprising for the modern reader is the mention of eating swans' eggs; indeed, it is probably illegal nowadays to buy them even if one could reconcile eating them after they had been boiled, shelled, halved and the yoke pounded up with butter and spices to form a paste which is then filled into the cavity of the white and gently heated. But it seems that even in Eliza's day the swan's egg was not widely known about, if we are to observe that Longmans thought it worth their while to commission an engraving of one as an illustration for the book that, as their Ledgers show, cost them 7s 6d to the artist concerned. Eliza gives a very personal footnote on swans' eggs, as well as a culinary tip in the receipt Swan's Egg en Salade, where she tells us that it is possible to achieve a perfectly smooth mixture by mashing the yoke on a dish with a broad-bladed knife. At the bottom of the page she confides that when she received her first present of swans' eggs she was staying in a house 'where there was no regular mortar – a common deficiency in English culinary departments'. Was it possible that when her book appeared, the shops selling cookware were besieged by keen cooks seeking to buy pestles and mortars?

Apart from receipts either given by or dedicated to actual people, Eliza took others from different parts of the country and, indeed, Europe too. So we get Kentish sausage-meat alongside the French sausage-meat cake or Pain de Porc Frais, and Tonbridge Brawn precedes Italian Pork Cheese. The latter name is interesting because the term 'pork cheese' was used in Suffolk instead of brawn. When it came to stews, the reader had the choice of German, Welsh or English. She also gave a number of receipts that used ox cheek, a meat that has currently enjoyed a revival in restaurants as well as in the more discerning households. The receipt for Swedish Herring Salad uses sour cream which, she notes, is not much to the English taste, though judging by the dairy department of our supermarkets, it has become so. The town of her mother's birth, East Farleigh, gives its name to a dish of fresh herrings; while Greenwich provides two receipts, one for dressing whitebait and the other, Water Souchy, made with flounders, perch, tench and eels, was the basis of the famous Greenwich fish dinners. The mention here of Greenwich raises the question, did she know the apothecary and his family at Greenwich Hospital who will be mentioned later in connection with Ann Kirby, Eliza's servant?

Westerfield White Soup has connections with Suffolk, too, the village being the home of the Edgar family who played such a big part in the Acton family's years in Ipswich. Eliza's observation on the soup shows us a rare glimpse of her personal life:

> We have given this receipt without any variation from the original, as the soup made by it – of which we have often partaken – seemed always much approved by the guests of the hospitable country gentleman [Milesom Edgar] from whose family it was derived, and at whose well-arranged table it was very commonly served; but we would suggest the suppression of the almond spikes, as they seem unsuited to the preparation; and also to the taste of the present day.

Today's readers, perhaps, would not only find the almond spikes a problem, they would be hard pressed to find the bone of a knuckle of veal which formed the basis of the soup.

'From the varied produce of a well stocked kitchen garden, it may be made excellent at a very trifling cost.' Eliza was a sensitive writer; she did not dictate that a certain item in a receipt must be included at all costs whether liked or not. For example, in her Sorrel Salad, to be served with lamb or veal cutlets or roast lamb, she starts by saying:

> This, though a very agreeable and refreshing salad, is not to be recommended when there is the slightest tendency to disorder of the system; for the powerful acid of the uncooked sorrel might in that case produce serious consequences. It should be especially avoided when dysentery, or other diseases of a similar nature, are prevalent. We mention this, because if more general precautions were observed with regard to diet, great suffering would, in instances, be avoided.

Having issued her warning and given instruction on how to prepare the tender young sorrel, she remarks: 'this fine aromatic herb is less generally relished in England than in many other countries; but where it is not disliked it may be used with great advantage in our cookery: it is easily cultivated, and quite deserves a nook in every kitchen garden.' That piece could well have been written for inclusion in Miss Acton's Receipts in one of the magazines to which she contributed. Her concern for the health and preferences of her readers is paramount, especially if she is recommending a dish which may be new to some, as, for instance, in the case of the Mullagatawny Soup which contained grated coconut: 'although the cocoa-nut when it is young and fresh imparts a peculiarly rich flavour to any preparation, it is not liked by all eaters, and is better omitted when the taste of a party is not known, and only one soup is served'. Similarly, Eliza was sensitive to kosher dietary rules. Without actually drawing attention to them, she made the comment in a footnote to the receipt for Old-Fashioned Mock Turtle Soup: 'When the butter is considered objectionable, the flour, without it, may be mixed to the smoothest batter possible, with a little cold stock or water, and stirred briskly into the boiling soup: the spices should be blended with it.' Eliza's Jewish friends would have made her aware of the taboo of mixing dairy products with meat.

Eliza's allegiance to Suffolk surfaces on numerous occasions, suggesting that she may have visited often during the time she was living in Tonbridge. She had, of course, her brother Edward and his family living in Grundisburgh and her sisters in posts in the county, as well as many old friends. It may be that when she discusses the well-known Bakewell Pudding she is recalling the dinner held following the ceremonial election of aldermen in Ipswich that she would have witnessed as a girl. Served on all special holiday occasions, this pudding was as famous in several northern counties as it was in Derbyshire. However, Eliza observes in a somewhat disapproving voice: 'This is a rich and expensive, but not very refined pudding. A variation of it, known in the south as Alderman's Pudding, is we think, superior to it. It is made without the candied peel, and with a layer of apricot-jam only, six ounces of butter, six of sugar the yolks of six, and the white of two eggs.' This recipe is, in fact, an adaptation of a mid-eighteenth-century one known as Ipswich Almond Pudding.

On occasions she indirectly imparts to us snippets of local history. For example, in her chapter on game she mentions the French or Red-legged Partridge. She does not give instructions on how this should be cooked, but merely remarks that provided the bird has been well hung and properly prepared, it will make good eating. What is interesting is her note that where this bird has been introduced into Britain, it has driven out the native grey partridge, which has made it 'an undesirable occupant of a preserve'. Introduced into Suffolk by the Marquis of Hereford to his Sudbourne Estate, near Woodbridge, these birds, rather than providing greater sport for the guns, had caused havoc among the native bird population and had led to the subsequent drive to exterminate them. One would not have expected a lesson on the dangers of upsetting the ecological balance of the landscape in a cookery manual, but then Eliza was not just a cookery writer.

In fact, Eliza was more in tune with the modern reader than we might suppose. Take, for example, her description of cakes as 'sweet poisons'. She has, she writes, only included a small number of cake receipts and would have gladly reduced that number had it not been feared this would cause dissatisfaction among her readers. So, she takes it upon herself to remark only that:

> more illness is caused by habitual indulgence in the richer, heavier kinds of cakes ... amongst those which have the worst effects are almond, and plum pound cakes ... all varieties of the brioche and such others as contain a large quantity of butter and eggs. The least objectionable are simple buns, biscuits [she means homemade ones] yeast and sponge cakes, and meringues; these last being extremely light and delicate, and made of white of egg and sugar only, are really not unwholesome.

Feeling as strongly as she did on the subject, it is surprising that she included among her limited cake repertoire Isle of Wight doughnuts, made with and cooked in lard as they were. Interestingly, she inserted a few currants into the centre of each before placing them in the boiling fat. Describing how the cooked doughnut should be left to dry on the back of a sieve, she imparts to us another nugget of social history. 'When they are made in large quantities, as they are at certain times of the year in the island, they are drained upon very clean straw.' Nothing is new; the burgeoning summer tourist trade was already demanding tasty take-away food.

SEVEN

THE LITERARY CIRCLE

I t was stated earlier that if we wish to learn more about Eliza Acton, then we have to search for clues among her writings. In the previous chapter we learnt something of her strong views on subjects such as nutrition; the waste of food and the suffering of the poor; the necessity to educate women, in particular in domestic affairs, as well as her reading and understanding of scientific matters. But a study of some of the names ascribed to receipts in *Modern Cookery* will reveal more of her personal tastes in the Arts and in books in particular. A piquant sauce, which Eliza observes as being particularly good when mixed with the brown gravy of a hash or stew, or served with game or other dishes, is said to be Christopher North's Own Sauce for Many Meats. It is perhaps entirely appropriate that a literary critic's contribution to her book should be somewhat tart in its composition. Under the pen name of Christopher North, John Wilson, the Professor of Moral Philosophy at Edinburgh University, was the leading writer and reviewer for *Blackwood's Edinburgh Magazine*. He was responsible for articles about, and reviews of, the work of most of the writers and poets of the first half of the nineteenth century. This very popular magazine would have kept Eliza informed about the publication of all new books, whether they were of fiction, poetry or scientific; foreign translations or original English, including American writers, as well as notices of the current theatrical productions, which 'Christopher North' considered of any worth.

It is, however, her choice of fiction that is interesting. Predictably for the period, she read the work of Charles Dickens. The modern reader, who may be daunted by the density of a Dickens novel, should remember that he too wrote for magazines and that many of his novels were produced in serial form. It was as a tribute to *Martin Chuzzlewitt*, which was serialised in 1843/4, that she adapted the original Beef-Steak Pudding à la Dickens, calling her refined version, in which she substituted butter for suet, Ruth Pinch's Beef-Steak Pudding after one of the leading characters. When *Modern Cookery* appeared at the beginning of January 1845, Eliza sent Dickens a presentation copy with an accompanying note. Her letter has long gone, but his to her has been preserved. Reading between the lines of his reply, we gain some idea of her tentative approach in sending him the book. Bearing the date of 11 July 1845, he wrote:

> I beg to thank you cordially for your very satisfying and welcome note of 10 January last and for the book that accompanied it. Believe me, I am far too sensible to the value of a communication so spontaneous and unaffected, to regard it with the least approach of indifference or neglect – I should have been proud to acknowledge it long since, but I have been abroad in Italy.

With the six-month delay in his response, Eliza would have been forgiven for thinking that he had been both indifferent and neglectful. But one suspects that Dickens did not really appreciate talented, independent women.

The novelist who may prove a surprise to the modern reader is Fredrika Bremer, a Swedish writer whose work was translated into English by Mary Howitt, herself a prolific writer and poet whose early work had appeared alongside Eliza's in Fulcher's *Sudbury Pocket Book*. Eliza read the early novels of Bremer when they were published in England in the first half of the 1840s, and must have been both intrigued and delighted to find a novelist who used food both symbolically and as part of the story's plot. Here was a woman after her own heart, so she approached Bremer by letter for details of some of the dishes. This resulted in Miss Bremer's Pudding, and Mrs Werner's Rosenvik Cheese-Cakes, which featured in the novel *The Neighbours*, being included in the first edition of *Modern Cookery*. The ensuing correspondence between the two authors showed just how much they shared in common; both were poets – strangely, in their younger days, both had developed the underlying theme of the power of the night – and both were keen cooks.

Although Bremer, who was only a year or two Eliza's junior, had been brought up in more affluent surroundings, her mother had insisted that she and her sisters were trained in superior domestic skills in readiness for the day they would become mistress of the home of their wealthy husband. But by the time the two authors began their friendship, marriage was no longer in the forefront of their minds. Instead, both had a keen interest in the economic, political and social condition of the world in which they lived and what they could contribute to help improve the lot of those less fortunate than themselves. And while Eliza drew inspiration from the novels for dishes to include in her book, I venture to suggest that Bremer later drew on Eliza for her depiction of certain aspects of character in her later novels. This is not the place to discuss the Bremer novels, but for their time they were extremely forthright in their view of the female role in society and that women should have the freedom to make life choices for themselves. The novel *The Colonel's Family* is surprisingly outspoken in its depiction of the damaging physical and mental effects of repressed female emotions and unrequited love; subjects which Eliza also explored in her poetry.

Eliza's generosity in readily assigning praise to others was not just mere flattery. Early in her acquaintance with the Swedish author, Bremer sent her the directions for a soup associated with her famous countrywoman, the singer known fondly as the Swedish nightingale who had drawn huge audiences to her concerts in London. The soup featured in the cookery book as Mademoiselle Jenny Lind's Soup, with Eliza adding the words – Authentic Receipt. It begins thus:

> This receipt does not merely bear the name of Mademoiselle Lind, but is in reality that of the soup which was constantly served to her, as it was prepared by her own cook. We are indebted for it to the kindness of the very popular Swedish authoress, Miss Bremer, who received it direct from her accomplished country woman.

In a footnote we are told that she had been informed by Miss Bremer that Mlle Lind was in the habit of taking the soup before she sang as she found the sage and eggs contained in it both soothing to the chest and beneficial to the voice. In one paragraph Eliza had managed to pay tribute to both singer and author and probably gained new admirers for both.

The warmth of feeling that existed between them can best be illustrated by part of a letter written by Fredrika Bremer on 21 October 1845.[20] Like Dickens she had been sent a complimentary copy of the first edition of *Modern Cookery*, and like Dickens she had taken a long time to acknowledge it. Her excuse that she too had been abroad has, however, the added extenuating circumstances that she had been in attendance at the deathbed of a dear friend. Her grief had been so great that at the time she had been unable to think of anything else, but now she had returned to her own home and was able to write. Although Bremer spoke English, her command of the written word was not entirely accurate. This is the second half of the letter as it was written:

My dear Miss Acton! You are one to which I address my most hearty thanks for the good will and amiableness expressed by your words and gifts. Your book is a far more delightful present than you are aware of, and some [of] its receipts are already copied, and 'Miss Bremers [sic] Pudding' and 'Mrs Werners [sic] Cakes' are by this time eaten by the Professors and fine Ladys [sic] of old Upsala[21] the seat of our old Gods. My mother is very curious about the Pudding and as soon as we will be, for the winter, settled in Stockholm she thinks to invite her friends to taste the pudding bearing her daughters [sic] name. As for your Violets [Eliza had given her a basket planted with her favourite flowers before she left England] the[y] will be a sweet smell to my nose but more so to my heart. O my dear Miss Acton! Those sweet perfumes reveeling [sic] the loveliness which blooms in the human heart are blessed spells for the soul who is doomed to experience much of the rottenness of life. And may God bless you for the generous disposition you have; and which prompted you to bestow on me loving words and gifts! But you are right to think that you do not bestow them on a stranger, I am indeed *the friend* of such as you.* This spring your Violets will bloom on the graves of my beloved

ones,[22] and for ever (so long as I live) they will be cherished in my own study.
My love and hearty good wishes remain with you;
I remain Your
   obliged and grateful
   Fredrika Bremer

Arsta 21 Okt

1845

* And to you and for you I have often talked in my writings and will talk still.
Readers as you warms the blood of the writer.

The exchange of letters was not simply one of politeness, a devoted
reader communicating her pleasure to an author and the grateful author
expressing her thanks. Their correspondence continued, perhaps somewhat
desultorily on Fredrika's part, as she was very busy travelling not only in
Europe but in America too. In 1851, the year of the Great Exhibition, she
turned her attention to England, spending a year touring the country in
preparation for a book entitled *England in 1851; or Sketches of a Tour in
England.* During this time she and Eliza must have met, but where or for
how long and under what circumstances is not recorded. But among the
Bremer archive there is a letter written following this long stay. It is such
a letter as could only have been written to one with whom one shared
an easiness of manner and a similar sense of humour. It is a delightfully
intimate letter despite the formal address, which, of course, was the usual
practice of the period:

Stockholm in May 1852:

Dear Miss Acton!
I have to thank you for your two little friendly notes, and to ask your pardon
for not having done so earlier! Yet I am sure you know I thanked you in my
heart for your kind words. Now let me tell you of the violettes [sic] that you
planted for me, and that I took with me as a parting present, from London.
[This had become Eliza's trademark!] The basket in which I put the two little
pots hardly left my arm during my travelling over sea and land till I came

home. As I wandered with it through a doorway in the 'Douane' at Calais in the dusk, an officer rudely enough, arrested [stopped?] me laying hand on my poor basket, and calling out: 'qu'estes-que c'estque ça? – Ah! je vois,' continued he removing a paper and looking at the two flowerpots and a bottle of Eau de Cologne and a little one with eau de rose, the contents of the basket, 'je vois. Du gibier, de la volaille, du vin! Bien, bien passez!' At which I could not help laughing right out and saying; 'non ce n'est pas du gibier, ce sont violettes!' at which my Argus looked rather piqued but said, 'c'est egal, passez!' And I passed but called afterwards my two little flowerpots 'Gibier et Volaille.' When I came home the poor little foreigners seemed not to thrive. Two plants died out by little and little. The other looked long as if they would follow. But at springtime one of them began decidedly to grow and develop new leaves. The other followed. And the other day 'Volaille' took me by surprise by opening a sweet blue-eyed flower. I made all the noses in the house bow to it, and mine again and again, [to smell its scent] in honor of Eliza Acton and her gift. Now the flower is passed, or I should put it in my note, but another [sic] is foll[ow]ing ...

Dear Miss Acton, as soon as my sister Charlotte, 'the lady Judge' will come back from an excursion in the country I will make her give me receipts for some very excellent Swedish dishes she is very 'bonne menagère', and I will send them to you.

And should you in my next romance find a lady who makes her fortune and reputation by making good things, and likes to spoil people by giving them good things, that they yet are very happy to get; – a lady whose sfere [sphere?] is all sweetness, a lady just to be put in a tale* – delightful for great and small children, – and yet a real lady, a sensible lady, whose only fault is that she will spoil her own stomach dealing so much in sweet things, but a lady after all that we could wish should live forever to make life more sweet and tasteful, – then, dear miss Acton lay it at the door of the inspirer not at that of the taleteller.

Yours

very heartedly

Fredrika Bremer

* as: il y avait une Dame a tartines dans un beau palais de beurre frais, etc.

This is a reference to the traditional French nursery rhyme:

> Il était une Dame Tartine
> Dans un beau palais de beurre frais.
> La muraille était de praline,
> Le parquet était de croquets,
> La chamberà coucher
> De crème de lait,
> Le lit de biscuit
> Les rideaux d'annis.[23]

This delightful, chatty letter almost rings with laughter as Bremer mentions her encounter with the Customs officer. From other writers of the period it would seem that travellers through Calais often found that the rather gruff officials did have a sense of humour.[24] This one, having asked what she had in her basket, had on inspection identified the flowerpots as being game and chicken, while the scents were branded as wine. When she corrected him, he dismissed her with a brief, 'It's all the same'. And in the references which describe Eliza as being sweet, is there just a hint of friendly teasing? If the word spelt as 'sfere' is meant to be 'sphere', could this be a little dig at Eliza's putting on weight? There is evidence to prove that the Bremer girls were brought up to be very weight conscious so there may be significance in the suggestion that Eliza's only fault was that she might spoil her stomach by too many sweet things. It is possible, however, that she was genuinely concerned about damage to Eliza's digestive system rather than a fear of obesity. Perhaps it was Bremer who gave Eliza the idea to call cakes 'sweet poisons'. But what warmth of feeling is contained in Bremer's tribute to Eliza when she suggests she could be the inspiration for a story, and when she calls her 'a lady that we could wish should live forever to make life more sweet and tasteful'! This letter is important, too, on another level, highlighting as it does the fact that educated women throughout Britain and Europe were able to use French as a common language. Bremer took it for granted that Eliza would know the French nursery rhyme to which she refers. If there was an English version of it, it is not one that has survived.

Bremer's energy and drive to find out about other ways of life was boundless. Through her various campaigns, both directly and also within the pages of her books, she was able to initiate changes for the good. One, which would have been of particular interest to Eliza, was the campaign to tighten the laws on the copyright of an author's work which, alas, came too late to save her from the later plunder of a certain Mrs Beeton, who, among many other receipts, took the Jenny Lind soup for her book, renaming it Soupe à la Cantatrice.

On the back of the 1845 letter but written in a different hand were the words 'with Mrs Howitt's regards'. Mary and William Howitt were a truly amazing couple. Their energy for life, as well as their prolific literary output, seems almost unbelievable to a modern reader who has a stereotypical picture of how life was lived in the nineteenth century. Mary was born in 1799, the same year as Eliza. But unlike her she married young. With her new husband, William, they embarked on a very varied literary career which encompassed poetry; stories and verses for the young, of which probably the most long-lasting of Mary's has been 'Come into my parlour, said the spider to the fly'. Individually and together they wrote stirring adventure stories, accounts of travels in far distant lands, and improving works of many kinds. Both Howitts were interested in encouraging the talent of other writers, particularly foreign ones, thus widening the scope and range of material available to English readers. Mary, who like most young ladies of her time had learned French and German, was quick to appreciate that here was a niche for her, and in the 1840s she was translating the work of both Bremer and Hans Christian Anderson from German into English. She was self-taught in Swedish and, as time went on, she eschewed the German editions and worked directly from Bremer's original copy. In the first chapter of her *Autobiography*, Mary explained how she came to know Eliza Acton. The piece is interesting as it not only gives several clues about Eliza, but also gives a taste of Mary's own style:

The far-famed citron-soufflé of the estimable Louise in Mdlle Bremer's novel, *The Home*, also procured for me a most agreeable and lasting friendship with an estimable, gentlewoman, Miss Eliza Acton. In perusing *The Home*, the soufflé had not escaped her observation, and she was anxious to obtain the exact receipt from Mdlle Bremer for the second edition of *Modern Cookery*. She was also desirous of information about 'sweet-groats' and other preparations for grain mentioned in *The Neighbours* as forming part of the national food of

Sweden; for she was much troubled by the culinary inaptitude of the English people. She had found that amongst the lower classes not one in ten could even make a loaf or boil a potato as it should be.

Mrs Howitt was writing many years after Eliza's death, but she offers us another rare tribute to her. Mary had had a very wide circle of friends and acquaintances throughout her long life but yet she remembered Eliza as someone who was a long and agreeable 'friend', not merely an acquaintance. For the Victorians the distinction was a very real one.

Mary, too, finds her way into *Modern Cookery* with a pudding known as Mrs Howitt's. As this is subtitled Author's Receipt, it may be that Eliza had made this pudding for the Howitts when they came to dinner one evening and, because Mary had enjoyed it so much, it was thereafter dedicated to her. To our eyes this is a version of bread and butter pudding, made with slices cut from a roll or a light bread, buttered on both sides and then spread thickly with orange marmalade. The difference is that the custard (properly prepared, of course) is flavoured with French brandy.

William Howitt made his contribution, too. In 1852 he set out with his two sons for Australia where his brothers had arrived twelve years before. Brother Richard remained there for some time before returning to England to write *Impressions of Australia Felix, during four years' residence in that colony*, which despite the length of its title was much acclaimed following its publication in London in 1845. The other brother, Godfrey, eventually settled with his family in Melbourne and died there in 1873. So when William and his boys arrived at Port Phillip in September 1852, they were not without contacts in the country. Four weeks after landing, they set off with one of Godfrey's sons to join those digging for gold. The life that they shared in the goldfields was recorded by William in his book, *Land, labour and gold; or two years in Victoria*, published in London in 1855. The book takes the form of a series of letters in which William describes what he witnessed with both a critical eye and a sharp sense of humour. Fortunately for us, one of these letters was addressed to Eliza. Again, it is in reply to a request she made to him either by letter or in person before he left England:

Bendigo diggings, Victoria Sept 6th 1853

Dear Miss Acton,

You asked me to write you a letter from the Australian Bush, and I promised
that I would; so here it is. I have, however nothing in the world to tell you that
you may not hear from Mrs Howitt ... [which suggests Eliza was in regular
contact with Mary] ... But as my doctrine is that promises are not made to be
broken, like pie-crust, but to be kept like a good cake or preserve, so I keep mine
... Perhaps you don't know this, however, that your book ... goes everywhere
with us, and has been most serviceable. When I come away I mean to bestow
it as a valuable present to my sister-in-law ... meantime we are continually
referring to it, and if we could find in it the materials as well as the mode of
cooking them, we should 'fare sumptuously every day'. [Describing the prices
of the limited food supplies available, he mentions that some of the families on
the diggings keep goats and fowls, and that had they access to her book they
might cook many good things.]

Chops and stakes [sic] and tea, with a few plain puddings are our chief fare.
We make famous bread, however ... not a particle of alum in it, except it lurk in
the flour. We make our bread with carbonate of soda and tartaric acid, muriatic
[hydrochloric] acid being much too quarrelsome stuff to carry about us.[25] It
is enough that we have serpents, scorpions and centipedes to contend with,
without having ourselves scalded, or our clothes destroyed with the smash of
a muriatic acid bottle. But no bread can rise better than this does, it often lifts
off the lid of the camp oven to look about it, it is so much puffed up with itself.

How Eliza must have smiled at that last description of the bread rising,
and she probably would not have been unduly upset by the mention of
the snakes and insects. Although she would have been interested in his
receipt for Leather-Jackets, bush tea might have caused a shudder; being
as it was tealeaves, strong brown sugar and water boiled up together in
the tea kettle, Howitt called it tea syrup. He tells her that he is alone in
camp at this time, his sons having gone ahead to the next camp to which
they were to move. He describes his daily routine. Having got a good fire
burning he starts on breakfast: '[I] season a steak in the frying-pan. I
flatter myself I could season and cook a steak to please even you – the
Queen of Cookery ...'

How delighted she must have been at that accolade and how well William knew what topics were of particular concern to her, such as the purity of bread. But the picture that is revealed from this letter is not that of a severe Victorian spinster in her fifties, but rather it is a tribute to Eliza's sense of humour that such a pleasantly relaxed relationship existed between them that William knew he could tease her. His teasing goes even further when, after apparently seriously suggesting she should write a bush cookery book showing what they might create out of almost nothing, he gets carried away with what could be done with kangaroos, opossum, bandicoot and wombat, before launching into cannibalism.[26] He concludes:

> It is now spring and many beautiful shrubs and flowers are coming out: for which see – My Book!
>
> I remain, dear Miss Acton Yours faithfully, William Howitt.

There could hardly be a greater contrast between the austerity of the Australian outback and the luxurious surroundings of the Gothic novelist William Beckford. Neither can there be greater extremes between the values held by Howitt and Beckford and the work they produced. If members of the upper classes are born with silver spoons in their mouths, then Beckford's must have been of the purest gold for he was heir to the richest man in England. He had every advantage that money could buy; for example, Mozart was his music teacher! Bright, talented, gay – in the current sense of the word – he toyed with the arts as gentlemen of the eighteenth century did. When exiled into Europe he travelled widely and, like Howitt was to do, wrote sketches of the places he visited. But it was earlier, in 1782, that he had written his best-known work, *The History of the Caliph Vathek*. Beckford wrote it in French but it was then translated and published in English without his permission in 1786. Its Arabian setting must have drawn audiences, especially those who relished the descriptions of the five pavilions dedicated to the gratification of the senses, the terrifying journeys and dark depictions of hell, while the moralists could take comfort that at the end there was no escape for Vathek.

It is perhaps arrogant of us to think that Eliza would not have read this book. We have, alas, been conditioned to think that in the 'olden days', nice young ladies did not read anything apart from improving literature. But we

have only to read Sheridan's *The Rivals* to learn that was not so. And Jane
Austen proved it also in *Northanger Abbey*, where she deliberately set out
to satirise the popular Gothic novel with which she, and later Eliza, grew
up with. So it is not at all surprising that Rice à la Vathek finds its way
into her book with the additional comment beneath the title of 'extremely
good'. It is indeed a luxurious pudding with its combination of almonds,
rice and large quantities of milk. The modern cook, however, might find it
exceptionally time-consuming to make and the result might not necessarily
bring gratification to the sense of taste.

An altogether different kind of writer, both in character and literary
output, was the country gentleman and cleric Richard Harris Barham,
who under the pen name of Thomas Ingoldsby wrote *The Ingoldsby Legends*,
of which probably the best known now is *The Jackdaw of Rheims*. That
the legends were written in verse would surely have appealed to Eliza, as
would the fact that he had the ability to impart both historical and literary
information to his readers with great humour. Who can resist the following
example, chosen at random, of his deadpan mode of delivery?

> The Captain is walking his quarter-deck,
> With a troubled brow and a bended neck;
> One eye is down through the hatchway cast,
> The other turns up to the truck on the mast;
> Yet none of the crew may venture to hint,
> 'Our skipper hath gotten a sinister squint!'

These are verses to be read aloud for the entertainment of friends and
families, and it would be pleasant to think of Eliza relaxing with her copy of
the edition which appeared in 1840. Barham's ancestral home, disguised
as Ingoldsby Hall, was Tappington Hall in Tappington Everard, near the
village of Denton in Kent on the Canterbury to Dover road. Eliza must
have known the Barhams well, for she certainly did not hesitate to request
special receipts from them for her book. The result was Ingoldsby Christmas
Pudding and Tappington Everard Receipt for Cherry Brandy, both of which
suggest she had been entertained at intimate family gatherings. The former
has been tried and tested by generations of cooks, many of whom will
have appreciated Eliza's advice in her observation that: 'A fourth part of

the ingredients given above, will make a delicious pudding of sufficient size for a small party: to render this very rich, half the flour and breadcrumbs may be omitted, and a few spoonsful of apricot marmalade well blended with the remainder of the mixture.' The directions for making cherry brandy are very similar to those followed nowadays in the making of, for example, sloe gin. Kent was the centre of the cherry-growing industry and good housewives preserved the fruit in many ways at the end of the harvesting period; in 1799 Nelson's wife, Fanny, used the fruit from the trees in her Ipswich garden to make the liqueur to send out to the Admiral. But during the nineteenth century, cherry brandy became very popular as a suitable drink for ladies. In *Cranford* Mrs Gaskell hints that ladies who engage in trade may consider it to be a sign of gentility. When Miss Betsey Barker retires from running her shop with sufficient funds to be regarded as a suitable person to be visited by the ladies of Cranford, she entertains them to an evening of card playing, before which she serves a more than adequate tea. After the cards she gives them not only a supper, the like of which had not been seen in their circle, but also persuades them to join her in a glass of cherry brandy. The ladies are not quite sure if they should imbibe, especially as they think it might contain alcohol. Such are her arguments for their trying – and even enjoying – the liqueur that Miss Barker shows that she has not lost her ability as a saleswoman.

It is unknown who was the accomplished scholar who provided Eliza with the receipt for Herodotus' Pudding. This, like many of the others, was a variation of a boiled pudding made from dried fruit, suet and breadcrumbs; this one, however, was laced with a good measure of sherry. Eliza observed that this receipt really was to be found among the work of Herodotus, the Greek historian from the fifth century BC, the only changes being the substitution of sugar for honey and sherry for the wine of ancient Greece. She adds that this was one of the dishes she had not tested for herself, but since the scholarly gentleman had had it served at his own table more than once, she accepted its authenticity. Greek scholar he might be, she could not resist doubting that the pudding needed to be boiled for the fourteen hours he had suggested. She believed half that time would be sufficient. That comment suggests that again Eliza knew the gentleman quite well and had eaten the pudding at his table, hence there was no necessity for her to test it for herself. There is also the suggestion that she knew him well enough to know that he would not be affronted by her publicly declaring in her pages that she disagreed with his cooking time.

Was Eliza having just the slightest dig at Mr Longman with The Publisher's Pudding? She opens the receipt with the words, 'this pudding can scarcely be made *too rich*' (Eliza's italics). It is, as many of her puddings were, a boiled one. The ingredients included both Jordan almonds and bitter ones; three-quarters of a pint of boiled cream was poured over the almond paste, which was pounded and then placed in a cloth in order to wring out the almond-flavoured cream. To this was added, among other things, crushed macaroons, the best Muscatel raisins, dried cherries, candied citron and a glass of the best Cognac brandy. It is an interesting receipt and one that readers might try for a special occasion. Eliza added the comment that if it were well made, it was very light as well as rich, and that without the almonds it would be sufficiently good for most tastes. When she included this pudding did she realise that her work was going to make her publisher even richer?

In contrast to the Publisher's, comes The Poor Author's Pudding. Unlike the long preparation and cooking time of the former, this is simplicity itself. Half a stick of well-bruised cinnamon, or the thin rind of a small lemon, is boiled in a quart of milk with 3oz of sugar & a few grains of salt. It is poured into a deep basin to get cold and, when it is, three well-beaten eggs are stirred into it. After being strained into a pie dish, the mixture is covered with half-inch-thick slices of crust-less bread, buttered on both sides. It is then baked in a moderate oven for half an hour. It is interesting to note the language used in this very simple bread and butter pudding, which speaks of the need to be economical. Half – not a whole – stick of cinnamon; thin rind from a small lemon; a small number of eggs and certainly no dried fruit or marmalade added. Eliza may have had to economise many times in her own kitchen while she was compiling *Modern Cookery*.

EIGHT

FAME AND FORTUNE?

For most writers, once their work has reached the printing stage their involvement with it is over. The idea that they conceived and nurtured within them for months finally emerges as a complete entity to be delivered up to the world for scrutiny and there is nothing more the creator can do for his progeny. For some, nowadays, there may be an initial flurry of radio and TV interviews with perhaps a local bookshop signing, while a major novelist or a television celebrity may embark on a round of lectures and signings throughout the whole country, with the addition of speaking engagements at literary festivals in order to promote sales of his book; but for the majority, once the book is written it must fend for itself while the writer gets on with the next one.

But things were very different for Eliza. Hardly had the first print run of *Modern Cookery in All its Branches* hit the bookshops when there was demand for the next edition. This meant that she was required to attend to any mistakes that had appeared in the printed copies, alter things and make additions. Longman promptly sold this second edition to the American publishers Lea and Blanchard of Philadelphia. Their advertisement for it advised that the book had been revised and prepared for American housekeepers by a Mrs Sarah J. Hale.[27] In her preface, dated August 1845, Mrs Hale stated that she had often been surprised to discover how far behind the times the United States was in the art of cookery. She had therefore been delighted to undertake the publisher's request to supervise the American edition of this new work of Miss Acton, especially when she found out how well it was adapted to the needs of America at that time. She then paid great tribute to Eliza's own preface saying that it was in itself complete as it explained fully the author's wishes and motives in publishing the book. Because the work was based solely on the author's own experience, Mrs Hale considered it would have been wrong of her to attempt many additions to it. What she had done was add items that referred chiefly to the preparation of those articles which were regarded as more strictly American, such as Indian corn, terrapins and some others. The only revisions she had made referred either to the use of a few English articles or of terms that were not generally known in the United States.

Lea and Blanchard had scoured the English press for suitable comments to include within the book to support their publication. Among these, *The Sunday Times* reviewer wrote:

> We have subjected this book to the severe test of practice, and we readily concede to it the merits of being a most useful auxiliary to the presiding genius of the cuisine. The instructions it gives in all that relates to culinary affairs are comprehensive, judicious and completely divested of old-fashioned twaddle. It contains, besides, some novel features, calculated to facilitate the labours of cookery, the principal of these is the summary appended to each receipt of the exact quantities of the ingredients it contains, and the precise time required to dress the dish. To the practical woman who seeks to combine comfort with economy in the direction of her household concerns, this book will prove an invaluable treasure.

This was praise indeed, surprising though it may be to find the phrase 'divested of old-fashioned twaddle' being used in 1845!

The American interest in health must have guided the selection of the following two reviews. *The Medico-Chirurgical Review* benignly stated: 'We cannot too warmly recommend to the notice of our junior brethren this compilation of Eliza Acton's, which will prove as useful to young Mrs and her cook in the kitchen as *Thomson's Dispensatory or Conspectus* to the young doctor in the library.' While *The London Medical Gazette* critic, who may have been a Scot given the form of address he adopted and his personal views on economy, wrote:

Mistress Acton writes well, to the point, and like a woman of sterling sense, her preface ought to be printed on a broadsheet, and taught to all young ladies at all boarding schools and all schools whether boarding or not, in England ... We add moreover that the receipts are all reasonable and never in any instance, extravagant. They do not bid us sacrifice 10 pounds of excellent meat that we may get a couple of quarts of gravy from it, nor do they deal with butter and eggs as if they cost nothing. Miss Acton's book is a good book in every way, there is right-mindedness in every page of it, as well as thorough knowledge of the subject she handles.

This really was a review worth having. Not only did the critic praise her literary style, he showed acute appreciation of what she was trying to achieve. What writer would not have been proud of this and what lady would not have relished being acknowledged as a woman of sterling sense?

The last reviewer touched on a subject that had generated much discussion over the years. From the time when meat, fish and fowl dishes for the rich and refined were introduced, they had usually been accompanied by sauces of varying thickness made of flour and butter with the addition of cream, milk or herbs. Gravy as an accompaniment developed by serving the actual juices extracted from the meat itself, though not quite in the way we know now. The great gravy debate came to the fore during the nineteenth century when it was realised that the customary method of making it was uneconomic and totally wasteful. Earlier chefs had recommended cooking vast quantities of beef purely to extract its juice, then discarding the over-stewed or over-fried meat. The more prosaic Mrs Rundell had at least offered some alternatives to good beef, suggesting the use of the cheaper cut of skirt mixed with ox kidney or the part of a shank of mutton that was not required for the table, making sure that the shank bones had been well soaked first. Her receipt for Gravy that will Keep a Week is a pointer as to what went on in most middle-class kitchens:

Cut lean beef thin, put it into a frying-pan without any butter, and set it in a fire covered, but take care it does not burn; let it stay till all the gravy that comes out of the meat is dried up into it again; put as much water as will cover the meat, and let that stew away. Then put to the meat a small quantity

of water, herbs, onions, spice, and a bit of lean ham; simmer till it is rich, and
keep it in a cool place. Don't take off the fat till going to be used.

Eliza entered the debate with her introductory remarks to her chapter on
gravies, stating that neither abundance nor variety was required for smaller
households, where 'a clever cook will manage to supply at trifling cost,
all that is generally needed for plain family dinners; while an unskilful or
extravagant one will render them sources of unbounded expense'. Then, in
one of her informative footnotes, she relates a cautionary tale: 'We know of
an instance of a cook who stewed down two or three pounds of beef to make
gravy for a single brace of partridges; and who complained of the meanness
of her employers (who were by no means affluent) because this was objected
to.' Eliza's culinary knowledge and experience gained during her stay in
France is now brought into play. Instead of frying the gravy ingredients as
was done in most English kitchens, French cooks 'pour to them first a small
quantity of liquor, which is reduced by rapid boiling to what is technically
called *glaze*'. Her method still required the use of a meat base, but often
her receipts included the addition of broths or soups that had been made
without meat.

It was during her discussion on the making of what she called a plain
beef gravy soup that Eliza revealed her interest in scientific matters. It is
obvious that she made it her business to read the articles which appeared
in scientific magazines, particularly those that in any way related to
nutritional matters. She was very interested in the work of the German
scientist Baron Liebig, who had used his knowledge to experiment on
how to prepare good gravy without incurring great cost. His receipt
needed a pound of good, juicy beef, preferably rump steak, chopped very
small, like sausage meat, mixed with an exact pint of water. This was
then left to stand at the side of the stove to heat very, very slowly for two
to three hours. Only then was it allowed to come gently to the boil for not
more than fifteen minutes. The resulting strained liquid then served to
provide that standby of invalid food which appeared so regularly in the
literature of the period – nourishing beef tea. Professor Liebig established
the principles of slow cooking in order to maintain both nutriment and
essential vitamins. Eliza was to recommend that this gravy should always
be used to convert cold, leftover meat into good, nourishing dishes instead

of the plain hash and mince prevalent at the time. The problem of what to do with leftovers she blamed on the English practice of buying far larger meat joints than was necessary. However, it was then up to the good cook to use her ingenuity to use the excess cold meat wisely and well. When discussing the invaluable beef tea, she maintained that it was important that every family should know exactly how to make it. Forestalling the criticism of the economist, who might regard buying rump steak for the purpose as expensive, she pointed out that 'drugs and medical advice are usually far more so'. Was she speaking here from her own personal experience of requiring medical advice and drugs? Certainly for us it is a reminder of just how much illness existed in that period – tuberculosis, for example, which was so prevalent among young people, who might linger in an invalid state for many months or even years, before death. Eliza, like most people in the nineteenth century, had seen many of those she loved taken by one disease or another, among them her youngest brother John.

And in 1847 John senior died. He was 71. His cause of death is not known, but given his age and the fact that he died in January it is more than likely that influenza or pneumonia was the cause. We last encountered John when he and Elizabeth were in lodgings in Grundisburgh on the night of the 1841 census. But for him, his life came full circle when he died in Hastings, the place of his birth. There is no documentary evidence as to what brought him and Elizabeth back there or when, but the 1851 census found the widowed Elizabeth and her daughter Catherine living in Denmark Place at St Mary in the Castle, Hastings. This was part of a splendid new complex consisting of a Palladian-style church and housing, and it has been suggested that her home was at 7, Pelham Crescent. All of this indicates that the Acton family fortunes had taken a turn for the better and that before his death John was again proudly styling himself as a 'gentleman'.

Eliza, of course, was earning her own money. The first payment of £67 11s 2d from Longmans in June 1845 was followed annually with increasing amounts: £162 5s 6d in 1846; £189 3s 5d the following year, and £83 5s 10d in 1848 when her share was cut from half to a quarter. By today's standards, a struggling author would find these amounts acceptable, but when the values are translated into modern terms the figures are very impressive.[28] Even when her shares had been cut to one-eighth in 1849 she was receiving £83 5s 10d; £59 5s 3d; and in 1850 her share brought her £40 12s 1d, which shows how well the book continued to sell. In 1851 Longman took the same step John Murray had with Mrs Rundell years before: he bought out Eliza's interest in the remaining stock and, more importantly, the copyright of the book for £300. However, unlike the breach which had occurred between Mrs Rundell and John Murray, Eliza appears to have continued on good terms with her publisher, for in December of 1851 she received a payment for her *Invalid Cookery*, and by 1855 she was busy editing the new edition of *Modern Cookery* for which she received £89 5s 0d. One may wonder what she did with her newfound wealth. Part of it could have allowed her to set up house in Hampstead, London, while the rest was probably invested in order to provide an income for her old age. In the 1851 census she is described as an 'annuitant', that is, living on a fixed income from an annuity. It is to be hoped that she took advice on how best to use her money from her Mercer relations who were well-established bankers in Maidstone.

Not only was she doing revision work on her book for Longmans, she also found herself in demand for magazine writing. While years before, in what must by then have seemed like another lifetime to her, she had contributed her poems to literary magazines, now editors wanted her fashionable receipts. Among these was Mrs Jane Loudon, a woman whose pen was never still. Some seven years Eliza's junior, like her she had started her literary career with poetry, producing *Prose and Verse* in 1824. In 1827 came a science fiction novel, published anonymously, entitled *The Mummy! A Tale of the Twenty-Second Century*. She continued writing novels until her marriage in 1830 and thereafter she worked in partnership with her husband. After attending lectures in botany, she wrote articles which reflected both her own interest in the subject as well as the developing interest in gardening among the middle classes, especially ladies. Her output was already prolific, but when her husband died she was forced to do even more in order to support herself and her daughter. Thus, knowing her market, she produced such works as *Plain Instruction in Gardening, With a Calendar of Operations and Directions for Every Month in the Year; The Villa Gardener: Comprising the Choice of a Suburban Villa Residence etc*; and *The Year-Book of Natural History for Young Persons*. These titles are as symptomatic of mid-nineteenth-century England, with its fast-growing population, flourishing industrial output and the constant demands of commerce and consumerism, as they were of late twentieth-century Britain. The world of Eliza Acton's childhood was changing rapidly. In Ipswich, for example, when she was a girl the wealthy lived alongside traders and shopkeepers in the town centre, and large, impressive houses were cheek by jowl with much smaller ones; but now the erstwhile traders and shopkeepers who were successful no longer lived over the shop, but moved out to new housing developments on the edges of the town. The expression 'they have moved up in the world' was literally true in any town which had originally nestled among hills. In London what had been countryside now became a suburban area full of 'Villa Residences'.

In December 1849 Jane Loudon began editing *The Ladies Companion at Home and Abroad*, a weekly magazine that covered other topics as well as gardening. In the third issue of Volume One, on page 42, appears 'My Receipt Book' by Miss Acton. It is not known if the two women had actually met or if each simply knew of the other's work. Neither is it known who contacted who with regard to the articles, though now that Eliza was a celebrity cookery writer, it is likely that Mrs Loudon approached her, knowing what a draw she was likely to be for the magazine. Fortunately, Eliza was not expected to meet a weekly deadline, so it was in issue ten, on page 144 – the pages of each issue were numbered consecutively in order to build into a complete volume – that 'Miss Acton's Household Hints and Receipts' next appears. Two further articles under the same title appeared in issues twenty-five and twenty-six.

A rival to *The Ladies Companion*, which in May 1850 had been taken over by Henry Chorley, was Dickens' *Household Words*, which among other things provided a useful vehicle for the serialisation of his own and fellow novelists' work. At this time Mrs Gaskell's work was enjoying great popularity and Dickens was keen to promote her. When one looks closely at these two it can be seen how they supported each other, with Mrs Gaskell in *Cranford* giving what nowadays we would call a 'plug' for *Sketches by Boz* and the latest issue of *Pickwick Papers* which had totally captured Captain Brown's attention while he waited for his train. Had he not been so engrossed he might have noticed sooner the child wandering across the track. He was in time to save her but too late to save himself. It has been claimed that Eliza Acton also wrote for *Household Words*. If she did she must have used a pseudonym, which seems most unlikely, because his account books with their comprehensive list of fees paid to contributors does not include her name.[29]

That vital source of information, the 1851 census, reveals that at the time it was taken, Eliza was in Hastings with her mother and sister. We need not assume that she was actually living there permanently, rather that she was on an extended visit which may have been caused by a bout of ill health. It appears that she had earlier consulted a physician in London, William James Erasmus Wilson, who by the age of 40 had established a major reputation for his work among the poor. Treating diseases such as scrofula, anaemia and blood poisoning, he had become recognised as the leading authority on skin complaints. He had realised how many diseases were the result of infected water supplies, throughout the country and in London in particular. That, along with the ever-mounting problem of sewage disposal and the severe overcrowding in housing for the poor where personal hygiene was scant, was the breeding ground for recurrent epidemics as well as constant medical conditions. When he wrote his book on skin diseases in 1854, he dedicated it to Edwin Chadwick, the great campaigner for clean water for all. Wilson advocated daily baths for his wealthier patients, with the use of Turkish baths, spa treatments and thermotherapy. He and Eliza had much in common in their attitude to the importance of good food, well cooked, and, like her, he frowned upon the excesses of the wealthy. It was said of him: 'He treated the rich by ordering them to give up luxuries and the poor by prescribing them.' And prescribing was what he did for Eliza. She must have written to him while she was in Hastings with a query about her medication. Wilson's reply is one of the rare archive letters to her still in existence:

> 17 Henrietta Street,
> Cavendish Square

May 25 1851

My dear Miss Acton,
Omit your present medicine and take that which I now send to you.
Attend to the bowels after your own way by cold water or in any other manner
you may prefer. I see no objection to your remaining at Hastings and I have

much hope in the plan which I am now putting you upon.
Let me know how the medicine suits you and how you are at the end of a
week.

I remain, my dear Miss Acton,
Very faithfully yours
Erasmus Wilson.

This letter, of course, gives no indication as to what was wrong with Eliza.
Given Wilson's specialism, she may well have developed a skin complaint
of some kind. It appears that Wilson's medicine, whatever it was, had the
side effect of causing constipation, which she was advised to alleviate with
a cold water enema. The manner in which this is mentioned suggests that
both condition and remedy were common at that period. Given Eliza's age, it
is feasible that she was acutely anaemic due to the onset of the menopause.
What is interesting is Wilson's remark about his having no objection to her
staying in Hastings. Had she asked if she ought to return to London to be
close to him for further treatment? That suggests that she was very worried
about her health and he was doing his best to reassure her. Alternatively,
did she want to get back to London but her mother was anxious she should
stay? If she could quote the doctor's opinion that she needed to be in town,
then she could leave Hastings with a clear conscience. Such is the way
with biography; one can read between the lines but never be certain of
an interpretation, though we can perhaps safely say that Eliza had left
Tonbridge and was now living in London.

Similarly, we do not know at what stage Eliza parted company with her
servant Ann Kirby. She surely must have been Eliza's right-hand woman
in the kitchen at Tonbridge and over the years must have been regarded by
Eliza as a close companion. But we need to turn again to the 1851 census to
find out what had become of her. And what a surprise her location turned
out to be. It had been anticipated that Eliza had recommended her to a post
in some large private house, the home perhaps of one of Eliza's friends or
a contributor of receipts. It was certainly a large and very grand building
where she was then in residence, but one that was totally unexpected. She
was the personal servant of John Whitmarsh, a widower of 61 with two
teenage daughters, Mary and Adelaide, and they lived in an apartment in

the Royal Greenwich Hospital where Mr Whitmarsh held the important position of dispenser, with at least two assistants. It is odd to think of Ann, who had spent her younger days in reasonably quiet surroundings, now living among all the doctors, surgeons and their wives, families and servants. There was a cook, of course, on the staff of the hospital to cater for the patients. Did she tire of hearing what Miss Acton had said or done, or did Ann remain aloof in the private apartment, keeping quiet about her previous employment? On the other hand, with Ann cooking for them, the Whitmarsh family must have eaten well.

One wonders how the rest of Eliza's family felt about her fame. Was there jealousy of her success or were they all too busy leading their own lives to worry about such things? Again, there are no letters to tell us how close they all remained to each other or how often they were able to meet. The one official piece of evidence we have is that of the census, which does at least tell us where they all were on the night of 30 March 1851 and gives some indication as to how their lives had changed over the previous ten years. By 1851 three members of the family were missing. Two were through death – John Theobald in 1836 and their father John in 1847. The third member, Edgar, who had gone to Mauritius, was not in a position to pay home visits on a whim, so contact with him would have been limited to letters and possibly the occasional ex-patriot visitor on leave from the island who would bring news of him.

We have already established that Eliza and her sister Catherine were in Hastings with their mother on census night. We know that Eliza was only visiting and the same may be true of Catherine. A superficial reading of the census could suggest that Catherine, like so many unmarried daughters at that time, was a permanent resident with her mother until Mrs Acton's death in 1855. However, the fact that Mrs Acton died at the home of her sister Charlotte Miller in Teston, in Kent, seems to suggest that Catherine was already employed as a governess, as she was in 1861, when we find her in a Yorkshire rectory looking after the children of the widowed Reverend Francis Tremlow's children.

While Eliza and Catherine were in Hastings in March, not far away from them, living in much more splendour in fashionable Brighton, was their sister Anna. She was still with the wealthy Corrance family, as she had been for a long time, at their home Loudham Hall, at Pettistree in Suffolk.

She had watched the children grow up and now her only charge was the 15-year-old Isabella. Aside from them, and Mr and Mrs Corrance and their 20-year-old son George, there were ten servants also living in Marine Parade to look after them. Given the length of time that Anna had served the family, one can perhaps safely assume that she was highly regarded by them as a companion and friend.

It is likely that the family had come to spend the season in Brighton; perhaps sea-bathing had been prescribed as health-giving for one or more of them. Certainly the family still retained connections with Suffolk, the eldest son eventually becoming Member of Parliament for East Suffolk. Many of the receipts Eliza used that mention Suffolk may well have emanated from the Corrance kitchens, suggesting that she visited Anna on numerous occasions, and it is probably not stretching the reader's imagination too far to suggest that during her stay in Hastings, the now famous author was invited by Mrs Corrance to the house in Brighton to meet her lady guests.

But there was a further link between the Acton family and Mr Corrance, who shared with Edward Acton a keen interest in archaeology. The year 1851 found Edward still in the Suffolk village of Grundisburgh with his wife Sophia and their five children, ranging in age from 12 to 19. He was still practising as a surgeon. Besides his private patients, for many years he also held the position of medical officer under the Poor Law for the Carlford and Colneis district.[30] But as time passed it must have been clear to those who knew him that his real interest lay outside the medical sphere, as he had become an avid collector as well as a contributor of articles on topics related to various branches of antiquities. While attending local meetings of like-minded scholars he would have met Eliza's old friend Mr William Whincopp, for whom she had written *The Reception*. During the eighteenth century, wealthy English travellers on the Grand Tour brought back relics of the treasures of Ancient Greece and Rome to enhance their great houses. However, the mid-nineteenth century seems to have inspired a tremendous desire among both the professional and leisured classes to delve deeper into the prehistoric past of their own country. Perhaps it was the result of commercial activity, the building of the railways, excavation for canals, the digging of mines, quarries and so on that had brought to the surface, quite literally, fossils and relics of great age. Few could afford an ancient Greek statue, but a glass cabinet

containing specimens of rock formations, shells that dated from before the
Ice Age, or fossils was possible and had the additional advantage of being of
educational value for the whole family, too, as suited the utilitarian spirit of
the age.

However, one display cabinet would not have been sufficient for Edward
Acton's wide collection. When he died in 1860, at the young age of 54, he
was described in his obituary as a 'Conchologist, Fossilist, Antiquarian and
Numismatist'. Much of his collection was donated to the British Museum.
Given their father's interest, it is not surprising that his son Walter became an
antique dealer in Brighton, while John, having been to sea, ended his career
in London as an antiquarian and dealer in works of art; only the eldest son,
Aubrey, was perhaps more influenced by his father's medical career as he
became a chemist.

Mary, with her elderly husband Anthony Gwynn, had by 1851 gone
from France to live in Grouville in Jersey, but by 1861 they had returned
to England to live in Reading. Their children, like those of Edward, pursued
some interesting careers, some of which illustrate the trends of the period.
For example, their eldest daughter Minna became an Anglican nun in the
Horbury House of Mercy run by the Sisters of St Peter the Apostle. With
the High Anglican Oxford Movement in full swing, a great many upper-
and middle-class single women found an outlet for both their religious
fervour and their desire to help others less fortunate by joining together into
sisterhoods and entering into communal living. The Horbury House started
as a rescue home for 'fallen women', an attempt to reduce the growing
number of young women who were forced into prostitution, and developed
into a huge complex which included the convent and its chapel, a hospital, a
retreat for clergy, as well as a school. Minna became Mother Superior of the
House by 1891. Her sister Mary also followed the religious life, as the wife of
the Reverend Henry Poole who emigrated to Australia, while the youngest
sister, Anna, devoted her life to nursing, becoming matron of the Royal
Bath Hospital in Harrogate before ending her career as matron of the Royal
Hampshire County Hospital in Winchester. She, too, was deeply religious and
is still remembered on the anniversary of her death in the mass said by the
Guild of All Souls, Little Walsingham.

Of the two sons, Anthony, who had been born in Grundisburgh in 1849,
possibly unexpectedly during his parents' visit to see Edward, spent his life

in the services, first in the Navy, then in the Royal Indian Marines. He appears in the census as 'Captain'. Tatham Gwynn, on the other hand, after matriculating at Exeter College, Oxford, entered the Civil Service. He married well and rose steadily in his profession, finally becoming Director of Naval Contracts in the Admiralty.

At the risk of this account of the careers of Eliza's nieces and nephews sounding like one of those ghastly family round-robins that occasionally accompany Christmas cards, we have to mention Helen Acton who married the entrepreneur Nathaniel Ogle, who with William Summers had developed a steam carriage in 1831. By the time of their marriage Nathaniel had lost his business, but recovered to become a director of several railway companies and other steam ventures both in the United Kingdom and abroad. He and Helen made their home first in Orpington in Kent and later in Twickenham, but by 1851 they too were living in Jersey, at Queen's Farm, St Saviour. One cannot help surmising that the Gwynns may have influenced the Ogles' decision to move to the Channel Islands; maybe Anthony had invested in some of Nathaniel's ventures. It would be pleasant to suppose that the young Ogles played on the beaches of Jersey with their Gwynn cousins, Tatham and Anthony being the nearest in age to Harmon, Catherine, Helen and Walter Ogle. Of these, Harmon became a clergyman, an Oxford academic and the headmaster of Magdalen College School, Oxford. Young Walter, on the other hand, may have been influenced by his cousin Anthony, for he eventually became a commander in the Royal Navy.

Having talked of Eliza's married sisters, let us now return to the last remaining unmarried one, Susannah. As the other girls had, she too became a governess. In 1851 she was living in Surrey at Milford House, Witley, the home of Robert Smith Webb, JP, a member of a wealthy aristocratic family. Her employer was a widower so in many ways Susannah became a surrogate mother to the four girls in her care who, in 1851, ranged in age from 17 down to 8. Like Anna, Susannah was living in a grand house with an indoor staff that included a housekeeper, butler, cook, a maid whose duties were confined to the schoolroom, kitchen and housemaids, and a pageboy. When she retired she joined Anna and Catherine in the house in Teston that had been the home of Aunt Charlotte. Following the deaths of her sisters in 1875 and 1876, Susannah was next found on the

Marriage certificate of Helen Acton

1881 census visiting 2 Priory Gardens, Folkestone, with an Edith Cooper, a lady of independent means. Susannah is described as 'Housekeeper'. This would suggest she was working still, perhaps for Mrs Cooper, but we need to bear in mind that she was now 70. In Aunt Charlotte's will, Susannah had, like all her siblings, received a legacy of £300. That she did not need to work is shown when, after her death the following year, her personal estate was worth £724 12s 11d. From her will we are given a hint that she had maintained contact with at least one of her nieces and nephews. Her sole executor was Tatham Gwynn, of 14 Delamere Terrace, Westbourne Square, London, Gent.

In answer to the question posed earlier, did the siblings resent Eliza's success, it would seem that the answer must have been no. Each of them made his or her own successful life; each would have gloried in the success of the others and each would have rallied to the aid of any one of them in need. With this large family of nieces and nephews, I cannot help querying again the story related by Aylett and Ordish that Eliza's supposed illegitimate daughter went to bed each night kissing a portrait of Eliza, saying that she was her real mother. Had Eliza had a daughter, I believe that she would either have acknowledged her as such at some point, or if she felt she could not go that far, then I am convinced she would have had her living openly with her as a niece or god-daughter, as Lady Hamilton did with Horatia Nelson.

NINE

THE 1855 EDITION

n the ten years following the original publication of *Modern Cookery*, Eliza must have been inundated with receipts from strangers as well as friends who wished her to try, approve and perhaps include them in some later edition. Thus it was that she was able by 1855 not only to add to the chapters she already had, but also to create new sections. And it is in these that certain ingredients occur which may surprise readers, ingredients that they will have supposed to be very modern. It has to be recognised that it was the impact of the two world wars of the twentieth century, with their blockades on foreign imports followed by financial restraints which resulted in acute shortages of essential foodstuffs, never mind luxury goods, that set English cooking back for several decades. The food rationing of the 1940s and '50s resulted in plain fare being the order of the day; it was a time when ingenuity was essential and nothing was wasted. The author has vivid memories of a birthday cake – a fatless sponge made with dried egg, covered with soya flour 'marzipan' and 'icing' concocted mainly from condensed milk. The highlight of the 'party' food was finger rolls spread with the deliciously sweet blackcurrant purée obtained in a small tin from the chemist. Small wonder then that when package holidays opened up the sunny shores of Europe in the 1960s, we became besotted with pasta and paella and all things foreign. And how very modern we thought we were when we tried to reproduce these dishes at home. The Swinging Sixties brought us coffee bars with their strange-sounding cappuccinos and espressos, frothy coffee with sprinkles on top served in cups and saucers made of toughened glass. For most people at that time, coffee was a thick black essence that came out of a tall, thin bottle with an interesting coloured label depicting a scene in an Indian Army camp. Ground coffee was a rarity in most households; it was expensive so only bought for special occasions, and then it posed the problem of how it should be made. To percolate or be placed in a sort of jelly bag hanging inside an enamel coffee pot? Either way it ended up being left to stew on top of the stove. How refreshing then to hear what Eliza had to say on the subject of coffee in England in the 1850s:

> There is no beverage which is held in more universal esteem than good coffee, and none in this country at least, which is obtained with greater difficulty. We hear constant and well-founded complaints both from foreigners and English people of the wretched compounds so commonly served up here under its name, especially in many lodging houses, hotels, and railway refreshment rooms*; yet nothing can be easier than to prepare it properly.

She then goes on to dismiss what she calls the elaborate and fanciful methods that had been suggested by some writers. Before she launches into the very detailed instructions for roasting coffee beans at home, and even longer instructions on how to make good coffee, she expounds on her footnote. Older readers will recognise that what she says was often true right up to the end of the twentieth century:

> * At some of the principal stations on lines connected with the coast, by which an immense number of strangers pass and repass, the coffee is so bad, that great as the refreshment of it would be of use to them, particularly in night travelling in very cold weather, they reject it as too nauseous to be swallowed. A little *national pride* ought surely to prevent this, if no higher principle interfered to do so; for to exact the price of a good commodity, and habitually to supply only trash for it, is a commercial disgrace.

It is tempting to add a footnote to Eliza's footnote on the subject of the development of the railway system in Britain, which by the 1850s had linked up the major towns and cities throughout the country. The lines connecting the ports along the east and south coast to London were of major importance in transporting the foreign tourists who came to visit the Great Exhibition of 1851.

If we wanted to hear Eliza's voice ringing out, what better example could we wish for than the tirade quoted above? This is Eliza, the patriot, ashamed that her country should present foreign visitors, let alone her own people, with – well her word says it all – trash. Then there is Eliza, the perfectionist, who believed strongly that whether it be a meal or a cup of coffee, it should always be presented in its finest form; finally there is Eliza, the economist, who could not bear to see money wasted.

However, when it came to buying coffee for home consumption, she recommended going to a first-rate London establishment and buying the finest quality, for, as she sensibly pointed out, it was a false economy to buy a cheaper coffee because one would have to use more of it to get the same strength; also, the flavour would be somewhat inferior. Coffee beans were always to be purchased freshly roasted and *never ready ground*. She then gives instructions for roasting beans at home as well as offering suggestions on the different types of coffee mill. She refused to have anything to do with the practice of adding chicory to coffee beans in order to deepen the colour, pointing out that some of the choicest coffee was of quite a pale hue. And how right she was in the admonition: 'Do not *in any way*, make use of the residue of one day's coffee in preparing that of the next; you would but injure the purity of its flavour ... and effect *next to nothing* in the matter of economy.' She points out that water poured onto the grounds of coffee that has been filtered will have very little taste or colour. It is probable that this last injunction was intended for the kitchen staff rather than the mistress of the house.

During the time she had lived in France, Eliza had learned to appreciate good, well-made coffee, which led her to have such strong opinions on the subject; for she has more to say about it, even going so far as to mention by name three London retailers. Indirectly, she also presents a picture of herself shopping in streets still familiar to us. While recommending the shops – did she get free gifts for her endorsement? – she was, as ever, honest in her opinion, anxious not to mislead her readers:

* ... By far the finest we have ever tasted we had on two occasions, some years since, from Mr Cobbett, of Pall Mall. The fragrance of it was too remarkable to be easily forgotten, and the flavour was exquisite, but it was apparently an accidental sample which he had met with in the market, for though very good, that with which we were supplied afterwards never equalled it.

Messrs. Stanforth & Co, 138, Oxford-street, are deservedly noted for the excellence of their coffee. It is always ground at the instant of serving it to a customer, and they have the complaisance of roasting even so small a quantity as two pounds, to suit the taste of the purchaser ...

The house of Messrs. Decastro and Peach, next door to Hatcher's Hotel, Piccadilly, may likewise, we think, be quite depended on for supplying genuine coffee to the public, and they have an immense demand for it.

In one's mind's eye, one can see Miss Acton seated beside the counter at Stanforth's, giving her order to the attentive assistant for beans to be roasted to her exact requirements, and one can almost inhale that bewitching aroma emanating from the roaster.

Far less appetising was what for a huge part of the English nation at that time was the mainstay of their diet – bread. Eliza believed that it, more than any other article of daily food, was that on which health depended. Yet it was almost impossible to obtain good, light, pure bread in England. Again, she had been heavily influenced by the French habit of bread freshly baked on a daily basis. Somehow the English as a whole had got it into their heads that making bread at home was difficult, so they bought it instead from bakers. In her opinion there was no reason why every cook and every female servant should not be able to make bread properly at home; pure, well-made bread which provided essential nourishment, rather than acting as a mere filler of an empty stomach. But in the nineteenth century the flour used in bread making was often full of impurities and additives, not least the mineral alum, and even, it was said, ground bones scavenged from churchyards put in to whiten the loaf. These additions had a deleterious impact on the health of the poor who lived almost entirely upon bread, even causing death among babies and old people. The accepted method of weaning a baby was to feed it pap, a mixture of crumbled bread soaked in milk with perhaps a knob of butter added to it. The alum acted as a purging agent on the child's digestion, causing acute diarrhoea which frequently led to its death. The very old and frail were often served pap with much the same result.

Once Eliza had started the section on bread, she realised that she had so much she wished to say on the subject that it would supplant the extra space she had been allotted for the new edition. There was only one thing she could do and that was to give her rules for making good bread with the inclusion of several receipts, one of which was the one she had devised herself for use in her own home and was called Bordyke Bread. All the facts and opinions she wished to impart to the nation about bread would have to wait until she had completed her next book, *The English Bread Book*. For it had been her intention that this revised edition of *Modern Cookery* should have a section on foreign cookery, under which heading she was to include Jewish cookery. Her concern was that if she dwelt too long on bread she would not be able to do justice to that subject in the space she had left, but she salved her conscience somewhat by pointing out that many of the tried, tested and guaranteed successful receipts already within her book had come, in any case, from foreign sources.

In actual fact, Jews would not have appeared at all 'foreign' to Eliza. Ipswich, during Eliza's childhood, was home to a sizeable Jewish community with a new, purpose-built synagogue and its own burial ground, which also served as the resting place for those of the faith who lived in other parts of Suffolk. The wealthier members of the group took their place in the social life of the town, alongside their Christian neighbours, while the rest engaged in trade, providing everything from the sale of silverware, allied with pawn-broking services, to greengrocers who imported the more exotic fruits. The retailing of ready-made clothes for the workingman, hats, toys, furniture and everyday household wares, along with second-hand clothing, all provided a living for Jewish families. The more artistic among them offered tuition in dancing, singing and the playing of musical instruments. Many of the community had settled in the parishes around the docks and it was in Eliza's own parish of St Peter that resided, in St Peter's Street itself, not far from the Acton family home in Dock Street, the most famous member of the Ipswich Jewish community. Sarah Lyons, whose descendants today are scattered far and wide throughout the world, was renowned for her longevity. When she reached the age of 101 in 1804, the aspiring young Suffolk artist John Constable painted her portrait.

No doubt an impressionable young Eliza would have seen the venerable old lady before she died in 1808. As time passed, the wealthier and more entrepreneurial Jews left the town, leaving behind those mainly engaged in the ordinary everyday trades with a smattering of professionals such as dentists, opticians and solicitors.

Once she was living in Tonbridge and later in London, Eliza would have met the ladies of the rich and influential Jewish families. Eliza was fully

The Ipswich synagogue, built in 1792. (Sketch copied by E. Cotton, from the collection of A. Copsey)

aware of the dietary laws governing a Jewish kitchen, particularly the taboo of mixing dairy products with meat at a meal, thus the use of oil when cooking fish, meat and vegetables. She also commended their use of ground almonds and rich sugar syrups in sweet dishes, which she believed preserved much of their oriental flavour. However, she added that she had been reliably informed, presumably by Jewish friends or acquaintances, that apart from those who were called 'Strict', that is, Orthodox, the majority of Jews in Britain did not rigidly observe the dietary rules. Perhaps it was for this very reason that *The Jewish Manual or Practical Information in Jewish and Modern Cookery* was published in 1846, a year after Eliza's *Modern Cookery*. Edited by 'A Lady', believed now to have been Lady Judith Montefiore, the book also contained valuable hints relating to the toilette; in other words, how to look after the skin, hair, nails and so on, with receipts for making beauty preparations at home. Although many of the dishes that appear in the two books bear a remarkable similarity, Eliza would not have spared space for advice on beauty care when she had much more important things to say on subjects like how to carve meat or cook vegetables correctly. What she had discovered to her great pleasure was Jewish Smoked Beef. She accorded it the accolade of 'excellent' written in italics, though it seems she quite missed the significance of what she was saying when she compared its flavour to that of a well-cured ham!

Apart from the flavour, the beef appealed to her sense of economy since it would keep well, long after it was cooked and cut, provided it was stored in a cool larder. It was also extremely versatile in that it not only provided a first-rate dish on its own, it could also be used to flavour gravies and soups. So impressed was she by the smoked beef, which, it seems, she had eaten at the home of a Jewish lady, that she asked for the name of the supplier. Interestingly, fulfilling the stereotype that Jewish tradesmen tended to live in London's East End, we discover that Mr Pass, the butcher, was to be found at 34 Duke Street, Aldgate. For the benefit of her readers who were unfamiliar with kosher practices: 'all meat supplied by Jew butchers is sure to be of first-rate quality, as they are forbidden by the Mosaic Law to convert into food any animal which is not perfectly free *from all* spot or blemish'. Could the same be said for the average London butcher of the time? Mr Pass also sold another item to which Eliza was partial, the spicy sausage chorissa. On reading how to use it, one cannot help being reminded of its similarity to the Spanish chorizo, which has enjoyed a prominent place in English cooking in the twenty-first century. The main difference is that the former is made of beef or chicken, while the latter contains pork. Is it possible that the Sephardic Jews adapted the Spanish recipe to their own purpose? And that when they were expelled from the Iberian Peninsula in the fifteenth century they took their version with them to Europe?

In this short section on Jewish cookery, Eliza lets drop that she was at the time also preparing a book on *Invalid Cookery*, which is mentioned in the Longman Ledgers for 1851.[31] One of the receipts which she intended for that book she decided should be included in this section because, as it contained no butter, it was considered suitable for the Jewish table. This New Baked Apple Pudding was, she declared, her own original receipt. Touchingly, she tells the reader that if her directions are followed to the letter, the result will be excellent, but any deviation will probably be attended by utter failure. One wonders how many times she experimented before she achieved a crust that was light, crisp and solid rather than turning to crumbs as soon as it was served. It is clear that Eliza had in mind not only those Jewish households which might wish to use her book, but also those hostesses who wished to entertain Jewish guests to dinner. So for their benefit she gives a brief lesson on those foods prohibited by the Mosaic Law, namely, 'pork in every form; all varieties of shell-fish, without exception; hares, rabbits and swans'. The last may seem surprising, particularly as we are all aware that swans are classified as protected nowadays, and most belong to the queen. Presumably, the general embargo on the killing and eating of swans was not in place in 1855.

From kosher kitchens in England we are next transported across the world for what might properly be called 'foreign' food, starting with a contribution on what Eliza called Tomata and other Chatnies, those being the accepted spellings for the period. This section is a timely reminder of Britain's imperial influence, particularly in the Indian subcontinent from the time of the establishment of the East India Company in the early eighteenth century. The adoption, and sometimes adaptation, of Indian dishes to suit the taste of the ex-patriot communities led to their receipts either being sent home or brought back by those retiring or on long leave. To someone living in the mid-twentieth century, reading Eliza's list from a hundred years earlier of items such as chillies, green ginger, green peaches, mangoes, ripe bananas, egg plant and roasted tomatas, mixed to a paste with salted fish, would produce nothing but amazement or disbelief. She had, she said, received all her receipts for the 'chatnies' from 'a highly intelligent medical man who has been for twenty years a resident in Mauritius'. It would be nice to think that this actually referred to her brother Edgar, whom we know went to Mauritius sometime after 1835, so that fits her description of 'resident for twenty years'. Certainly Edgar had been reckoned to be a very good scholar, winning his place at Oxford, so he could be her 'highly intelligent man', yet the fact that he left Oxford without a degree and moved to Mauritius implied that he was under some sort of cloud. However, it is possible that he had decided that the academic life was not for him and that like his brother Edward he would rather be a doctor. Eliza's reference would also suggest that if this is Edgar, then members of the family were in regular correspondence with him.

Eliza had other correspondents who had either lived in India or travelled widely. A friend who had lived for years in India gave her the receipt for A Real Indian Pilaw, while a mutual friend acquired for her the Simple Turkish or Arabian Pilaw from Mr Lane, famous in his day as the Oriental Traveller, but best known to us as the translator of the stories from *The Arabian Nights*. Before leaving the subject of curries, Eliza offered two receipts for making Bengal Currie Powder, making a slight reduction in the amount of black pepper used in the first, as she believed it was too coarse in flavour to suit English taste.

From India she moved closer to home with European receipts, the first being a risotto. This Italian dish has had a resurgence of popularity at the end of the first decade of the twenty-first century, though not every cook heeded Eliza's injunction that rice should always be perfectly cooked. Her second Italian dish was Stufato, a dish from Naples. We may recoil at a receipt that requires 6lb of silverside of beef cooked in 4lb of butter, to which is then added 3lb of pipe macaroni – and it appears that Eliza did too. She quotes the receipt exactly as she received it, telling her readers that it was given to her by a friend, at whose table the dish was served with great success to some Italian diplomats. So, indirectly she has confirmed that she had friends who moved in quite high circles, but at the same time she is critical of the methods employed in making the dish, not least that 3lb of macaroni was far too much to be served at an English table; her exact word being 'gigantic'. Several Austrian and German dishes complete this short foreign section, the last one being Mai Trank, a drink offered to visitors on May Day. This combined one pint of white wine to two of red, sweetened with sugar to which was added slices of orange and a bunch of the plant woodruff. Left covered to stand, it would be ready to serve the following day. For the modern reader the interesting point about this, apart from the use of the less well-known woodruff, is Eliza's comment that Rhenish wine should really be used, but 'this is expensive in England'.

And that was that, as far as Eliza was concerned. She had done all her corrections, she had added all the new receipts and the manuscript was ready to go to the printers, when there occurred every writer's nightmare – a new piece of information turned up. Did she consult Mr Longman as to whether she might have an extra page or did she simply go ahead and add the Salzburger Nockerl regardless. She tells us: 'at the moment of going to press, we have received direct from Vienna the following receipt, which we cannot resist offering to the reader for trial, as we are assured that the dish is one of the most delicate and delicious soufflé-puddings that can be made.' From the layout of the receipt it seems that she copied it exactly as she received it. In her author's note she informs us that this was so; the directions had been written by the physician in Vienna at whose table the soufflé was served. As she clearly had not had time to try this out for herself, the fact that she makes detailed comments on the actual serving of the dish suggests that she had been present in Vienna when it was served. By including this receipt she has indirectly thrown a tiny glimmer of light on her life outside the kitchen. How tantalising it is that we are not told when, or under what circumstances, she had visited Vienna. And we are left with the question of the identity of the physician. Was he English or Austrian? Was Eliza a friend of his wife? Was her visit to the house a one-off occasion or was she paying a longer visit? Or could it be that the relationship with the physician was a professional one and that Eliza went to Vienna for the sake of her health, which we know had given her cause for concern in 1851.

There was one final piece to be written before the new edition of *Modern Cookery* was ready for its public and that was the preface. Nothing offers more evidence of the intensity of Eliza's view of the state of the nation than this. Her preface to the 1845 edition had been designed to sell her book. By convincing the British public of the necessity to train its cooks thoroughly, she had the optimistic hope that once the population was made aware of this, well-prepared nutritious meals would be the order of the day, and the nation's health generally would improve. The preface on that occasion was, in many ways, simply a statement of what she intended the book to achieve. It is personal in the sense that she talks about the methods she has used in compiling the book, yet in a way it is also impersonal. She uses the authorial 'we' throughout, possibly to cover those who had helped her, but more likely as an alternative to the more personal first person singular.

How very different then is the new preface. As we read it one can feel her rising exasperation, nay anger, that nothing had really changed in the past ten years. She does not spare her readers; her opening sentence states that there is still a great need for a better understanding of the basic principles of domestic cookery, but what has really angered her is the unbelievable daily waste of perfectly good food. This evil, as she calls it, has been exacerbated by the appallingly high level of poverty among those engaged in heavy manual work, whether in factories or on the land, who struggle to find even sufficient bread to keep them alive. The starvation that followed the failure of the potato harvests in Ireland in the years 1846–8 had brought home to many in England the real plight of the poor. Now, in 1854, as she thought about her preface, Eliza read reports in the newspapers of the unrest throughout the country precipitated by a 30 per cent increase in food prices in the month of January alone. In one town, on one day, 300 hopefuls had queued up for entry to the workhouse, not one of them in a position to feed a family. The severe winter with its heavy falls of snow had made work impossible for agricultural workers, as well as workers like the 'navvies' who were engaged in digging out the tracks and tunnels for the ever-expanding network of railway lines. If there was no work, there was no pay. On the other hand, there was an exceptionally good export market to be had for British cereals, which meant that the price of bread at home had risen; the standard quartern loaf (3½ to 4lb in weight), which was the staple diet of working men and their families, originally costing fourpence was now ninepence, almost a day's pay, while the price of butter had jumped overnight from 1/- a pint to 1/4d.[32] Small wonder then that the starving poor tried to raid bakers' shops, and when they found themselves thwarted, turned into an angry mob rampaging through towns venting their wrath on shops and private property alike. The soup kitchens set up by charitable townsfolk, using some of the discarded or wasted food of which Eliza talked, provided only a temporary relief; they were not a solution to a very real problem.

It was her strong belief that an even greater evil was all the unnecessary diseases such as scrofula, scurvy and rickets, to name but three, that were caused through poor diet; whether from a lack of food, eating the wrong foods – that is, those that lacked any real nutritional value – or good food that had been ruined by poor cooking. Advances had been made in the understanding of what constituted a good diet by scientists of the period, in particular the chemist Baron Liebig, who had made a study of nutrition, but this knowledge had yet to be followed by the general public. It was clear that Eliza had read the scientific papers and may even have attended lectures on the subject. In this new edition, in a bid to educate as many people as possible on the right way to do things, she tells her readers she has taken advantage of some of these scientific suggestions, adapting her receipts accordingly, particularly those where it was possible to cut costs:

> for it may be safely averred that good cookery is the best and truest economy; turning to full account every wholesome article of food and converting into palatable meals, what the ignorant either render uneatable, or throw away in disdain. [It is likely that she was particularly thinking of the very wasteful habit of over-stewing expensive cuts of meat just to produce gravy.] It is a popular error to imagine that what is called good cookery is adapted ... to the wealthy, and that it is beyond ... those who are not affluent. On the contrary ... it is of the utmost consequence that the food which is served at ... the tables of the middle classes should all be well and skilfully prepared ... as it is from these classes that the men principally emanate to whose indefatigable industry, high intelligence, and active genius, we are mainly indebted for our advancement in science, art, literature and in general civilization.

At a time when many women, writers in particular, were espousing the cause of the poor, lobbying churchmen and politicians to improve their lot through education and religious teaching, good housing and clean water, Eliza had cast herself in the role of champion of the middle classes. Yet she was right to suggest that the professional men who were responsible for the industrial, commercial and artistic success of the country needed to be in the best of health to carry out their duties. How this was best achieved

may have come as a shock to many, as it went against the whole practice of
general household dining, yet it is among the recommendations given for
modern diet regimes:

> when both the mind and the body are exhausted by the toils of the day, heavy
> or unsuitable food, so far from recruiting their enfeebled powers, prostrates
> their energies more completely, and acts in every way injuriously upon the
> system.

To add emphasis to her argument, she says that she is not exaggerating
the case, 'for many a valuable life has been shortened by disregard of this
fact, or by the impossibility of obtaining such a diet as nature imperatively
required'. Neither is she talking about rare or extreme cases, she is speaking
from specific knowledge, 'and the impression produced on me by the
discomfort and suffering which have fallen under my own observation, has
rendered me extremely anxious to aid in discovering an efficient remedy for
them'. Was she talking here of herself perhaps, bearing in mind that the
letter from Dr Wilson mentioned earlier suggested both constipation and
stomach disorder? Or was it that, as most of her friends and acquaintances
were among the middle-class professionals, she had ample opportunity to
observe the large, rich meals they ate in the evening and to take note of
those who suffered illnesses as a result.

Her solution to this was to set out for her readers a healthy way of
preparing the simple and essential kinds of nourishment which formed
the staple of daily fare. She realised that 'elegant superfluities or luxurious
novelties' would have looked more attractive in the book but would not
have been as useful. To the readers who might be disappointed that she had
not included the 'fashionable dishes of the day' she reminded them that
those could be bought from the shops of competent confectioners. Instead,
she had used the space she might have allotted to such frivolous things to
the more homely subject of how best to cook and serve vegetables, and
for making good, unadulterated bread, a subject she had already touched
on. The third 'homely' subject is more surprising, namely 'those refreshing
and finely flavoured varieties of preserved fruit which are so conducive to
health when judiciously taken, and for which in illness there is often such
a vain and feverish craving when no household stores can be commanded'.

She then issued a dire warning against the eating of shop-bought preserved fruit, which she claimed was either adulterated in some way or so sweetened as to prove distasteful to invalids. No doubt she had proof that she was correct in her claims.

In her next short paragraph she again showed her irritation, this time with what she saw as a general lack of understanding about the purpose of food.

> Merely to please the eye by such fanciful and elaborate decorations as distinguish many modern dinners, or to flatter the palate by the production of new and enticing dainties, ought not to be the principal aim, at least of any work on cookery. 'Eat – to live' should be the motto, by the spirit of which all writers upon it should be guided.

And then we hear the true voice of Eliza. She can no longer hide behind the impersonal 'we'. She knows that what she is about to do is not at all what was expected of her, but it has to be done – and thus she reveals another reason for her growing anger:

> I must here obtrude a few words of personal interest to myself. At the risk of appearing extremely egotistic, I have appended 'Author's Receipt' and 'Author's Original Receipt' to many of the contents of the following pages; but I have done it solely in self defence, in consequence of the unscrupulous manner in which large portions of my volume have been appropriated by contemporary authors, without the slightest acknowledgement of the source from which they have been derived. I have allowed this unfairness and much beside to pass entirely unnoticed until now; but I am suffering at present too severe a penalty for the over-exertion entailed on me by the plan which I adopted for the work, longer to see with perfect composure strangers taking the credit and the profits of my toil.

The paragraph concludes with a reference to the original preface which told of the work taking ten years and all that had been involved in preparing the material for the book, work which was, she said, 'toil so completely at variance with all the previous habits of my life, and therefore, injurious in its effects'.

In the ten years between the two prefaces, more than twenty-five new cookery books had been published in Britain and well over half that number again in the United States which were also readily available in Britain. It stretches the imagination to believe that all these contained original work, so we must assume that a large number of them borrowed heavily from Eliza's book. And even worse were the pirated editions purporting to be her work. Publishing had become a cutthroat business. Mary Howitt, in her autobiography, recalled how in 1841 she and her husband had undertaken to print and publish Fredrika Bremer's early novels at their own expense as no London publisher would touch them. Then 'such became the rage for them, that our translations were seized by a publisher, altered and reissued as new ones. The men in our printer's office were bribed from America and in one instance the pirated sheets appeared before those we ourselves sent over.' As we shall see later, Eliza was spared witnessing Mrs Beeton's betrayal of her, her death coming but a few months before the publication of the first instalment of *The Book of Household Management*. Clearly Eliza's income had suffered from the fall in sales as other works appeared, but most galling to her was the fact that receipts over which she had toiled long and hard to perfect were now being passed off as the creations of others. She says that she had put up with the situation without comment – until now. Was it just loss of income that was worrying her or was there another reason? She might well have been mourning the loss of her mother who had died only a few months earlier in January 1855, but reading between the lines, this outburst suggests that Eliza's own health was suffering. That her physical health had given her concern in 1851 we already know, but it appears that as she wrote she was under both mental and physical strain. Any monetary concern would be alleviated when she received her cheque for £150 from Longmans for editing the new edition, but that would not necessarily ease her condition.

The truth seems to be that Eliza was weary; weary of her own physical limitations but most weary of having failed to achieve all the aims set out in *Modern Cookery*, the principal one being to instruct the complete novice by giving explicit instructions based on dependable and tested receipts. And in doing so, she would have helped tackle the problem of unnecessary waste. But this had not happened. Even though, she says:

a rather formidable array of works has issued from the press, part of them from the pens of celebrated gastronomers; others are constantly appearing, yet we make but slight perceptible progress in this branch of domestic economy. Still, in our cottages, as well as in the homes of a better order, goes on 'the waste' of which I have already spoken. It is not, in fact, cookery-books that we need half so much as cooks really trained.

She continued her argument that good cooking, and with it good nutrition, should be available to every member of English society and in that respect we were to look to our Continental neighbours and learn from them; not adopting their methods just because they were foreign, but adopting from them what was good. But that alone was not enough. She was somewhat heartened to see the increase in the number of cookery schools, but these still only produced cooks who went off into highly paid employment. It was these cooks to whom she looked to impart their knowledge to others in the future. Eliza might well have been even more depressed about the situation as she saw it had she been able to look forward 150 years. Nowadays, the trained professional cook is employed in large public establishments, such as restaurants, hotels, hospitals and care homes, with only very few in large private houses. The bulk of domestic cooking falls upon the women of the household, but with most of them also working full time outside the home, it is often easier to rely on ready-made or quick meals to feed the family rather than cooking a meal from scratch. Interestingly, more men than ever before now cook in a domestic setting, it often being the case that when two young people set up home together, it is the man who takes on the cooking. Eliza's plea for cookery schools was, of course, for domestic servants, but perhaps the time has come to reinstate Domestic Science into the curriculum of secondary schools. In the past, even the grammar schools of the 1930s onwards made sure that every girl, including those destined for university, training college and professional careers, had a year of domestic training that taught them how to make basic dishes as well as some needlework and laundry care. In the meantime, those modern chefs and cookery writers who have absorbed Eliza's teaching methods are doing their best to pass them on to the public – though, as Eliza found, not without some opposition.

By May 1855, Eliza had done all she needed to do to bring *Modern Cookery* up to date and was ready for the new edition to join all the others now flooding the market. In comparison with many of those it was expensive, at 7s, especially as a number were retailing as low as 1s. That her work was still considered to be a leader in the field of cookery books is proved by the review that appeared in *The Gardeners' Chronicle* of December 1856, which Longmans appropriated for use in advertisements for the book:

> A much enlarged edition of this useful collection of receipts. The preface seems particularly worth attention; it deprecates the waste so common in kitchens, yet shows good cookery to be desirable for persons of limited income as well as for the wealthy.

In many ways, the source of this review was significant; the growing of vegetables to supply the table had long been the prerogative of the grand houses with their kitchen gardens, while the agricultural worker might also grow a few basics in his back garden. Urban dwellers had to rely on shops and market stalls for their supplies, the freshness of which could not always be guaranteed. On the whole, the English were not great vegetable eaters and those they did eat tended to be over-cooked. But by the mid-1800s, attitudes were changing, particularly among the middle classes who moved to suburbia, where the sizeable gardens attached to their large villas gave them the opportunity to apportion part of that land into a vegetable plot. The development of the commercial glass industry, which had been displayed in all its glory in the building of the Crystal Palace for the Great Exhibition in 1851, meant that heated greenhouses were now within the reach of the more affluent middle classes. The doctor, the bank manager and other professional men could now grow a grapevine under glass as well as tomatoes, cucumbers and other salad items, and, most importantly, extend the normal growing season for fruit and vegetables. His wife could then happily fill the conservatory he had built on to his house with exotic plants, reproducing her very own miniature Kew Gardens.

With all this new interest in growing fruit and vegetables, Eliza had felt it necessary to instruct her readers on how they should be cooked. She had enough scientific understanding to know that the wrong treatment could destroy the value of a vegetable or fruit. Freshness was the key. Only artichokes were said to improve with keeping for two or three days, but all summer vegetables really ought to be 'dressed', that is cooked, within a few hours of being gathered. If that was not possible then she prescribed the best ways of keeping them from wilting. It is here, more than anywhere else in Eliza's book, that we are faced with the difference in our times. She was living in an age without refrigeration, but she did have, as did all middle-class houses, a cold larder. The one she mentions had a brick floor, others had flagstones. These rooms off the kitchen, for rooms they would certainly seem to us today, often being larger than the modern kitchen, were often north or east facing, with only a very small window that could be opened but had an inner covering of wire mesh to prevent the entry of insects. Shelves, usually wooden ones, though one at least might be of marble, lined three of the walls, and on one of them might be stored asparagus, cucumbers or marrows with their stalk ends placed in containers filled with an inch or two of water to keep them fresh. Other vegetables were to be spread out on the cool floor. However, all was not lost if the cook failed to do any of this; the remedy was to place the item in cold water for some time to refresh it. The downside of this was that the vegetable would still taste in Eliza's opinion 'very inferior'. When it came to general rules for cooking vegetables, Eliza was highly critical of the method she termed 'crisp, which means, in reality, only half boiled, [it] should be altogether disregarded when health is considered of more importance than fashion'. Her reasoning was that semi-cooked vegetables were not simply unwholesome they were also indigestible. She offered two further tips which are still worth following: first, that only dried peas and beans, Jerusalem artichokes and potatoes should be put into cold water at the start of cooking, while every other vegetable should be placed in plenty of fast-boiling water; second, they should never be allowed to remain in water once they are done – visions of watery, almost colourless cabbage and Brussels sprouts come to mind – because all the nutrients will now be in the water, which is probably why in living memory cabbage water was used to make gravy. Instead, Eliza recommended that the vegetables be well drained using a warmed strainer – sensible advice should your sieve be made of metal.

Her receipts for vegetables include some that may be strange to us. She used spinach, sea kale and asparagus widely, but mentions that should spinach not be available, her readers could go out into the highways and fields and pick young dandelion leaves, which, when cooked, she compared to endive.

She also mentions their medicinal properties. More surprising, perhaps, is her receipt for the roots of young dandelion cooked and eaten with melted butter or served with a cream sauce. How many gardeners today with a glut of young radishes would think of boiling bunches of them for eighteen to twenty-five minutes and serving them on toast? Stewed lettuce may be a step too far for the modern reader, but it is certainly worth looking at Eliza's receipt when the reader's vegetable plot is crammed with bolting lettuces. We discover that what she calls Windsor beans are known to us as the broad bean, and the modern cook tired of serving vegetables in the same boring manner may be surprised to find that Eliza shows much greater versatility, not least with nine different ways to present a cucumber!

TEN

THE LAST ATTEMPT

't's the greatest thing since sliced bread' became a catchphrase in the
1960s when, along with all the many other exciting developments in
our daily lives, bread not only came wrapped, it was cut into uniform
slices ready to make perfect sandwiches or fit into a toaster. It was, of
course, the fault of the Second World War that sliced bread, having made
its appearance in the 1930s, had been replaced by the standard off-white
National loaf which at one stage even had to be rationed. It is a chastening
thought that most of today's population will not have experienced the
childhood joy of the thick-cut 'doorstep' smothered in jam, or the thin
wafer slices served when visitors came to tea. Mastering the bread knife so
that the loaf remained straight rather than veering to one side or curving
inward was an art in itself. How much easier it became when a visit to a
supermarket, where the shelves were stacked high with hygienically
wrapped, mass-produced, machine-made loaves, took away the need for a
bread knife.

Of course, we had to admit that these loaves did not always have the
texture or flavour of those bought from the local baker, who could also offer
variety. So, when the mood took us, we sought out the local bakery. But not
often enough, and eventually, the craftsman who had served us faithfully
found himself forced to close his business and we no longer had choice.
With the passage of time, people tired of the ubiquitous sliced loaf and a
trend started for home bread making – with a machine, of course – while

the supermarkets realised that nothing beats the smell of baking bread to get the taste buds working and installed in-store bakeries which offered a wider variety of bread. And, as so often happened with food in Britain, some of those breads were the result of foreign influence; for example, with the different types from Italy, and more recently with the migration of workers from Eastern European countries, we have been introduced to breads made from cereals rather than wheat.

The failure of bread to live up to the expectations of its consumers is an age-old one. Disappointed with her failure, as it seemed to her, to improve the national standards of English domestic cooking, and struggling with her own ill health, Eliza took on one last challenge, that of improving the health of the nation through a radical change in the way bread, that staple of British diet, was produced. We know that while she was editing the 1855 edition of *Modern Cookery* Eliza had been frustrated that she could not expand what she wanted to say about bread, and it must have been then that she started planning the new book. Those who had welcomed her *Modern Cookery* must have been shocked when *The English Bread Book* appeared in 1857. This was not the anticipated receipt book, containing basic instructions for producing a good-quality household loaf for general use with the addition of a variety of loaves for different occasions. Eliza, the young woman who had started her career as a teacher, seen herself as a poet and literary figure, who had almost inadvertently become an accomplished cookery writer, now reverted wholly to the academic teacher she might have been in another generation. For *The English Bread Book* is a serious, scientific study and is much darker in tone than her previous work. It is also a treatise on the state of the country in the mid-1850s, a time when yet again acute poverty and starvation was fomenting restlessness and riot among a section of the population, and there was a general shortage of some foods resulting from the British participation in the Crimean War.

Eliza presented all this in a carefully crafted piece of writing in which every sentence had been executed to achieve the greatest impact. Note, for example, the balance of this from the preface, where she writes: 'Bread ... being in part the food of all – the chief food of many – and almost the sole food of many more.'

The title page says it all:

THE
English Bread-Book

FOR DOMESTIC USE

ADAPTED TO
Families of Every Grade:

CONTAINING THE
Plainest and Most Minute Instructions to the Learner;

PRACTICAL RECEIPTS

for Many Varieties of Bread;
WITH
Notices of the Present System of Adulteration,
and its Consequences;

AND OF THE
IMPROVED BAKING PROCESSES AND INSTITUTIONS

Established Abroad.

Her professed aim was that this book was intended for everyone, no matter what their class in society; though it quite clearly was not, and it was to be a practical book which would give simple and explicit directions as well as a variety of receipts for making good bread at home. But, and this is where the book differed from a straightforward cookery book, it was to reveal the truth about the adulteration of the bread the reader was in the habit of eating and, if that was not enough, readers were also to be warned of the dire consequences to their health of eating the accustomed slices. Since bread was such an important part of the daily diet, it was essential that:

everything which related to its consumption or economy is of real importance
to us; and it might naturally be supposed that the art of preparing it *well,
wholesomely, and without waste,* [Eliza's italics] would be an object of peculiar

household interest in families of every degree throughout the kingdom; and
that a familiar and complete acquaintance with its details would be considered
absolutely indispensable in the practical domestic education of all classes to
whom it is likely ever to prove useful.

William Howitt and presumably others of his class who had ventured out
to the gold fields of Australia were among those to whom the later part of
that sentence might apply. However, Eliza concentrated on those at home,
who 'seem so unaccountably opposed to our having really good bread made
in our own homes'. She believed that all that was needed was a little well-
directed effort and energy, and the eradication of the idea that making
bread was both difficult and troublesome. Unfortunately, in this present
age when everything has to be labour saving and quick, this fallacy still
persists. Perhaps it needs some celebrity guru to extol the therapeutic value
of kneading dough; anger, frustration and tension all disappear as one's
hands achieve the magic of creating that smooth ball which will become a
loaf. In Eliza's words: 'the instructions ... will serve to show how simple and
how facile the operation is; and if they become independent of the industry
and skill of others, for the preparation of the most valuable portion of our
daily food, the great aim of the author will be attained.'

There is something almost heart-rending in that aim. It is as if she felt
she must achieve this as the culmination of her life's work. Nevertheless,
she was not naive enough to believe that she could convert every woman
into a home baker, nor indeed that she should put the commercial baker
out of business. She was realistic enough to know that not every woman
had the time to bake bread weekly, let alone daily, and she was well
aware that in her plea for home baking, there was a large proportion of
the population which did not have access to an oven in the vicinity
where they lived, let alone one in their own home. She hoped that by
underlining this lack, she could influence those responsible for designing
and providing new housing for the poor. Eliza's aim was not just to
introduce housewives to good, home-baked bread; for the sake of them
and their families' health it was essential she should reveal the horrors
that existed in the world of the large commercial bakery. Not the small
local baker in the village or small market town, but the big bakeries in the
growing industrial areas.

She launched into her subject by reminding her readers how fortunate they were to live in a country that was justly famed for the purity and excellence of the grain that it grew. She then paid tribute to the work done in the agricultural industry, often at great expense, to achieve this high standard of corn, which in turn produced bread with such a pleasant flavour that it never palled on the palate. Bread was, she said, almost like an essential required by nature; whenever it was scarce and the price prohibitively high, the poor would seek alternatives, yet as soon as they were able, they always returned to bread. On the subject of price, she bewailed the fact that from beginning to end, grower to retailer, the final product, a loaf of bread, had to pass through so many hands, each taking excessive profits, with taxation adding to the toll. It was wrong that the entire weekly earnings of poor, hardworking men should be expended on bread alone, especially when the bread they were forced to buy did not nourish them, as it should.

What follows shows that Eliza was not merely one of those Victorian middle-class women who professed concern for the poor and did her bit practically on a very local level. In writing this book, Eliza intended that it should reach those who had it in their power to make changes.

> The usages and abuses of the bread-trade – of which I find myself compelled to speak, though I do it with the utmost unwillingness – tend in a measure to augment this misery, which it might sensibly relieve if its operations were conducted on the principles of sound reason and strict integrity, by saving the time of those whose lot is to labour incessantly for the means of existence; for it is a precious commodity to them, – a fact which philanthropic theorists do not always keep sufficiently in view when they are suggesting plans for bettering their domestic condition.

We are hearing here the same strong voice of the author who had felt compelled in the 1855 preface to expose those who had plagiarised her work. She is a woman with a mission and she speaks her mind forcibly, bravely taking on those 'philanthropic theorists' who waffled with ideas while she offered practical advice.

She then drew attention to the fact that the bread made by the current fermentation method produced loaves that were not sufficiently sustaining for those engaged in manual work, especially that performed outdoors. This bread quickly became dry and unpalatable, which in turn led to the temptation to wastefulness by it being discarded; waste, that is, of both the bread and the money it had cost. Add to that the tendency to adulterate the flour by the addition of other materials, plus giving short weight in the loaf itself, and the lot of the poor became even worse. So what could be done? Eliza's answer was that first and foremost the quality of the loaf should be the purest possible, and to achieve that meant a complete overhaul of the bread trade. The second important change needed was one to which she had referred in *Modern Cookery*, namely that 'such true practical education must be given to the female children, and to women of the working orders', in order that they might make bread in their own homes. But before they could do that it was essential that these women were furnished with domestic appliances in their homes. And in one of her footnotes she explained that often in entire small villages there was not one oven! That this was so seems unbelievable today, but if the village was too small to support a baker, then it was true. Even in towns like Ipswich, during the early part of the nineteenth century, those who could afford a roast dinner on Sundays, but were without an oven, were known to leave their joint of meat in its roasting tin at the baker's on their way to church, collecting the cooked meat on their way home, thus utilising the heat still in the bakery oven after the night's batches of loaves had been cooked. But for the poor who lived in tiny tenements or single rooms in a communal house, their only means of cooking was a pot over a small fire.

Having become political in her references to the need for ovens, and thus indirectly the poor housing conditions of vast numbers of the population, Eliza reinforced her arguments by quoting at length from William Cobbett's book *Cottage Economy*, published over thirty years earlier in 1821. The fiery radical had had much to say about the parlous state of England as he saw it during his countrywide tours.[33] Eliza must have read the book carefully and critically, for she commends it as a work, 'portions of which will be valuable for their clearness and sound sense', although she also comments on his forceful and direct style: 'Mr Cobbett, in his wish to impress forcibly on the minds of his readers the facts he set forth, is sometimes rather more vehement in his expressions than the occasion demands.' On the subject of home bread making she was somewhat more tactful than Cobbett, who declared: 'As for the art of making bread, it would be shocking indeed if that had to be taught by the means of books. Every woman, high or low, ought to know how to make bread; if she do not she is a mere burthen upon the community.' He could not understand how the situation had come about that women should be so ignorant of such a simple thing as making a loaf of bread, commenting that what was even worse was that many women seemed 'to know no more of the constituent parts of a loaf than they know of the man in the moon'.

Eliza makes it clear that she is disheartened that many of the sound suggestions Cobbett had made thirty years earlier had not been adopted. She points out that Cobbett was referring to the general lack of knowledge in his time, yet in spite of the fact that they were now supposed to be living in a period of great progress, ignorance appeared to persist even more than before. What would Eliza have made of those twenty-first-century children who have little knowledge of how milk is produced or even the main source of their beef burger?

But she had no time for crystal gazing, her aim was to rectify the evils of her own time and she started with waste. Where Cobbett had given complicated calculations on the price of wheat, the amounts of flour produced from it and so on, Eliza states simply that the annual waste of the finest corn turned into inedible – and therefore discarded – bread could have fed thousands. Leaving aside for a moment commercial bakers, she turns to the best starting point for improvement, and in one of her excellent footnotes advises:

> If the first question to a cook, on her application for a place, or to a general servant professing to cook 'in a plain way' were 'CAN YOU MAKE GOOD BREAD?' and her services were invariably rejected if she could not do so, there would soon be infinite improvement seen in this respect. Many modern cooks seem to think themselves absolutely aggrieved when they are required to perform this part of their duty, and assert, with an offended air, that they did not *engage to do it when they were hired!*

Rather than Eliza talking from her own personal experience of cooks, this suggests she had collected information from many 'aggrieved mistresses' who had put up with temperamental staff. One can imagine that whenever she found herself in the company of other ladies, the conversation would invariably turn to their domestic problems in the hope that she might be able to offer advice. Similarly, she would gain by listening to their complaints, especially if they added fuel to the arguments she wished to propound in her book.[34]

Arguing the point about waste, she said many people would think that the solution to the problem would be to buy bread only from bakers, where it was always good. It was difficult to convince those of the upper classes, who were in the habit of eating small, fanciful loaves of delicate texture, lightness and colour and made to perfection, that there was any basis to the claim that there were malpractices within the bakery trade. For the upper classes, whose daily diet consisted of an abundance of rich food, bread played such a miniscule part that it would hardly matter if it were pure or not. 'The grievous wrong of gross adulteration and of short weight falls the most oppressively on the very poor – often on those surrounded by half-famished children, for whom their utmost efforts can scarcely procure the means of life.' Having made this statement, she bravely took a risk by suggesting in a footnote that the very poor are forced to buy their bread from the 'most unscrupulous order of bakers, by some of whom, it is to be feared, they are cheated without mercy'.

She then turned her attention to the opinion of foreign visitors who found English bread very different to what they were accustomed. They complained that not only did it fail to satisfy the appetite, it also played havoc with their digestive system, the result of adding alum to whiten the bread. Consequently, discerning foreigners tended to seek out brown rather than white loaves. Eliza then displays her great knowledge of the history of bread making in France by quoting from two articles entitled 'Boulangerie de Paris' taken from the *Journal des Débats* of 6 and 27 January 1855. She read these articles in the original French and having studied them carefully she then devoted six pages in her book to how bakers in Paris had operated under the strictest controls from AD 630 onwards. It was a subject that interested her greatly, and one to which she intended to return at a later date as she indicated in the final sentence of a chapter dealing with the controls in Paris: '... but as these affect the interests of that one city only, they are omitted here, at least for the present.' Was she already looking for a future reprint with additions?

It was in the next chapter that Eliza, for the first time since her early poetry, makes a passing reference to religious belief. Discussing the adulteration of bread, she remarks that in a neighbouring country, presumably France, bread is often called 'the blessing of heaven'. She writes that the plain facts are: 'The earth yields us – thanks to a beneficent Providence – abundant food of the purest character, exquisitely adapted, if we use it rightly, to the healthy maintenance of human life; and we are assured, on high scientific authority, that it is so tampered with in its preparation for sale, as to become a positive vehicle of diseases of a most painful nature.' She has already stated that questions had been asked at the highest level, that is, the House of Commons, about the effects of adulteration but that opinion had varied, it being a case of scientific opinion versus commercial concerns. She found it hard to believe that the public, having been fed false information, should allow it to continue. Then she becomes almost militant with the rallying cry of: 'Let it be at once distinctly known and felt that the English people insist on being supplied with bread of genuine quality, and *they will have it*.' The italics are hers and that phrase could almost be a threat even though she tries to temper it by saying, 'they can effect – and with the utmost gentleness, if they will – any reform of the kind on which they are seriously resolved'.

She realised that it was wrong to blame the present generation of bakers for faults that they had learned during their apprenticeship to the trade. She was also sure that among them there were many upright and honest men who would never consider fraudulent practices. However, there was no doubt that most bakers, and millers too, denied that the alum they mixed with flour to produce white bread had any ill effects, despite the arguments to the contrary by medical men. She then added: 'Now, as their education generally does not qualify them to form an opinion worthy of respect upon the subject, it is unwise of them to make such an assertion.' Having written that, she either thought about it, or had it pointed out to her that this was a very sweeping statement, so to mollify the situation she added a footnote that read:

From the laborious and exhausting nature of their occupation, which is carried on through the night as well as in the day, the bakers, as a class, have perhaps less opportunity for self improvement than the members of other trades. They seek naturally too for some slight relaxation, when they have a little cessation of their toil.

The reference to self-improvement reminds us of the great movement for learning at all levels in the Victorian era, with the introduction of Mechanics' Institutes, for example, which provided lectures for the working man on a wide variety of subjects; Reading Rooms in villages; and the development of Penny Libraries in towns. For those who had had a basic education there was no limit to the knowledge that could be acquired by the diligent adult.

Eliza had not, however, finished with the subject of the injurious effect of alum. Having no doubt done so herself, she indirectly suggested that her readers should try the experiment to test the *excessively astringent* nature of alum. Placing a particle of it 'on the tongue will, in a moment, render evident to the utmost incredulous person – [it] must unavoidably have a very detrimental effect when it is taken, day by day, even in minute proportion, on the constitutions which are not unusually robust'. She again shows how much research she has done into the subject by quoting from Dr Ure's *Dictionary of Chemistry*; again, not a book with which we would have expected the average middle-aged, middle-class woman of the period to be familiar.

The book, which had been published in the 1820s, had highlighted the disorders caused by the introduction of alum, which included dyspepsia, stomach acidity, heartburn, headaches and palpitations, as well as a number of other conditions that were more acutely painful and dangerous which perhaps she thought it better not to list. Instead, she moved on to a discussion of the debates which had been held in the House of Commons on the subject of adulteration not only in food, but in drugs, too, the latter disgrace leading to the medical profession being unable to control epidemics or offer drugs of the right strength to effect a cure for a sick patient. The parliamentary debates were reinforced by her reading of the papers of the relevant Government Committee and scouring all the national newspapers for any report that might add support to her campaign. In doing so she was able to highlight specific cases such as that of the workhouses in Lancashire, where the flour that had been delivered to them from suppliers was found on analysis to contain, in addition to the wheat, 74 per cent of potato starch and maize flour. Another custom was to purchase wet or damaged flour, dry it in a kiln and then mix it with a little good flour and pass the whole lot off as being of first-rate quality. Items such as this roused Eliza to anger and she tells her readers of some of the punishments, mainly by public humiliation, that had been meted out in the past in France to those who had deliberately defrauded by adulteration of any kind, adding that at the time of writing the French imposed fines and imprisonment! Her next, somewhat surprising, sentence shows just how deeply she felt about the matter. 'In England the law deals even more leniently with such culprits, *pecuniary* loss being the only punishment allotted to them.'

England, she continued, may have prided itself on the tremendous progress that had been made in many branches of industry, which had justly brought it admiration from other countries, but when it came to the manufacture of bread, it was lagging behind not only France, but Belgium and parts of Germany, too. So strongly did Eliza feel, that she decided it was necessary to pass on to her readers some of the things she had learned from her reading and at the meetings of learned societies. The true voice of the author has been mentioned before, and here, without any apology, Eliza's own words are included at some length that the reader may 'hear' what she had to say:

I insert some of the details – unattractive as they are – without softening them for the fastidious reader, because any disgust which they may inspire will be a natural and healthy consequence, and may awaken a desire to aid in their abolishment. It is not well to shut our eyes, and determine to ask and to see nothing of evils which more or less affect life itself; though thousands of irreflective persons prefer to do this, rather than to investigate and endeavour to remove them. Many do not even *choose to believe* that the water supplied to the inhabitants of London requires purifying before it can be drunk with safety; or that the imperfect sewerage of that mighty city, so taints and loads the air with disease, as to render it often deadly poison to those who inhale it. So it is with regard to the bread they eat. They do not wish to be disturbed in their belief that it is all that it ought to be; and they treat as pure fancy, or prejudice, the idea that it can disagree with anybody, or be productive of serious and painful disorders. The common mode of making it is too well known to admit of contradiction. It is thus not very invitingly described by a foreign contemporary: it will be asked by our descendants, with astonishment, if indeed it could be true that, at this epoch of industrial progress, our principal aliment were prepared in the gross manner that it is, by plunging the arms into the dough, and raising and tossing it about with such force as to exhaust the strength of the half-naked journeymen, [trained bakers working for a master] and cause streams of perspiration to flow and mingle with the alimentary substance?

Reading these harsh, unvarnished truths, it is hard to reconcile their tone with our picture of the gentle instructress with a keen sense of humour that we have from Eliza's writing in *Modern Cookery*. Yet if we think back to her poetry, we can see that the same intensity of passion she displayed then for her broken love affair has been rekindled in her passionate crusade for better bread for all. If what she had said had not deterred her genteel, middle-class lady readers with its talk of sweat and naked men from continuing to read on, then there was still more to come. At this distance in time one cannot help wondering if Eliza was so incensed by the subject that she felt she had to reveal the facts as they were; or did she, perhaps, rather enjoy knowing that she would be shocking the sensibilities of some?

If instead of being satisfied with the aspect of the loaves exhibited in the windows of the bakers' shops, we were to descend into the offices where they are made, and witness the want of cleanliness and wholesomeness which attend their fabrication; could see *here* a reservoir of water which is never changed; *there* supplies of flour exposed to the influence of an impure atmosphere, either too damp or too overheated; and above all, sickly, perspiring men in contact with our food, we should turn away with a very legitimate feeling of disgust.

She describes the scenes so vividly that we are almost compelled to believe that she has witnessed them for herself. Perhaps she did, but if she did not then she certainly made good use of the descriptions given by those who had. She goes on to state that it is not the bakers themselves who are to blame for what she called 'these revolting pictures'. They are not responsible for the conditions in which they have to work. 'How can the air of the ill-ventilated underground premises ... be otherwise than most unhealthily foul, destructive to the men employed in them, and having the worst effects on the food which they prepare?' She hammers home the point that the one article of our nourishment, which depends in its preparation on purity and the utmost cleanliness, is lacking in both. A few lines further on she refers to an article she had read in the *Courrier de Lyons*, from 16 February 1854, which dealt with a new invention called the *Appareil-Rolland*, which, it was hoped, would supersede the current method which produced water-logged loaves. The writer of the article stated:

> In the middle of the nineteenth century bread-making is still a cruel labour!*
> The closed knuckles must be violently thrust into a huge mass of tenacious dough, which must be raised by the muscular effort of the arms, and turned and tossed over repeatedly with the most violent exertion ... Every part of his body is soon overflowing with perspiration which falls into large drops, and is amalgamated with the dough he is kneading; and he is entirely overwhelmed with fatigue by the time he has reached the end of his killing labour ... The further sufferings of the unfortunate workman, from the fine dust which he constantly inhales, and which is said to cause various pulmonary infections, from the manner in which it clogs the lungs; and the destructive effect on the eyesight of the burning atmosphere, which he encounters when placing his bread in the oven ...

Just in case she has overstated her case and put off prospective home bakers, the footnote Eliza appends states:

> * This applies only to bread-making on an extensive scale. There is nothing very laborious in preparing it in small quantities for domestic consumption.

In France, Monsieur Rolland, an experienced baker himself, had finally completed the experimental work of others to produce not only a machine in which the dough was perfectly mixed and then kneaded, but also an oven 'of a truly novel and ingenious description':

> It is heated externally [as opposed to the usual method of faggots placed in the floor of the oven] by means of hot air conveyed from a distant fire: the admission of smoke or other impurities into the interior being thus prevented.

The floor is a moveable platform, which can be raised or lowered at pleasure, and which turns on a pivot, put in motion by a winch, so that every part of it can be brought round in succession to the opening, and filled with bread, without recourse being had to the awkward, long handled peel [baker's shovel], which is of necessity used for ovens of common construction. The roof is not vaulted, therefore the loaves receive a more equal degree of baking than they do under the old system; and they can be watched through a pane of glass fixed in the door of the oven, the light from the strongly reflected flame of gas being thrown upon them.

Eliza seemed to give her wholehearted support to the Rolland oven, even going so far as to quote all those who had used it to their satisfaction. These included not only those in France, but even a Monsieur Delmehae of Rio de Janeiro, who spoke in the highest possible terms of the oven he had had constructed from plans, directions and models sent to him from France. More testimonials came from Venice, Vienna and 'a long array of other foreign cities'. These were intended to be the final words of the chapter, but after a suitable space comes the following, somewhat endearing, note from Eliza:

In the slight description of M. Rolland's oven which I have attempted to give ... I find that I have made a mistake in saying that it was heated by means of air 'conveyed from a *distant fire.*' The door of the furnace is placed quite away from that of the oven, but the fire is under it; and the hot air is made to circulate *over* and *round* it; by means of flues, which branch off from the main conductor in different directions.

Here is the voice of Eliza, the perfectionist, the writer/instructress who must be as accurate as it is possible to be; but also the woman who is not afraid to say 'I made a mistake'.

In her next chapter Eliza deals with a subject that has come to the fore very much in the twenty-first century, as a proportion of the population throughout the world has been found to be allergic or intolerant to products that contain gluten. For those who are not sufferers, the word 'gluten' was relatively unknown until recently, so it came as a surprise to read Eliza extolling the virtues of this substance called gluten, of which it is partly composed that gives to wheat its superior value to every other kind of grain as bread-corn, and renders the flour derived from it easily convertible into light, elastic dough. It does not contain a large proportion of this element – not more, on an average, than ten parts in a hundred, but this is in the highest degree nutritious; and its nature is such, that bread cannot readily be made from corn in which it is wanting.

Again, Eliza quotes at length from a lecture given in 1852, and a pamphlet on the subject which had appeared in the *Journal des Débats* on 30 July 1856. She also lets her readers know that she has read the work itself in the original French, but that: 'I give rather the strict sense and spirit than a literal verbal translation of parts of this article, which is somewhat diffuse.' Was she herself becoming somewhat bogged down in the subject? She does relieve the situation slightly by introducing an interesting sidelight on an alternative use for gluten. Quoting from Professor Donovan's *Domestic Economy*, we learn that from its glutinous quality 'it acts as a cement for broken glass and porcelain', and we could add that flour and water paste still offers many young children their first opportunity to stick cut-outs into a book or make Christmas paper chains!

One cannot help wondering how many of Eliza's readers, having ploughed their way through the chapter on gluten, were still with her when, in the following one, she continued to discuss Professor Donovan's work on how to remove the taint of must from wheat; the drying of wet grain, and bread made from germinated grain. A useful tip here was to mix 20–40 grains of shop-bought carbonate of magnesia to 1lb of flour. This would make the dough rise well in the oven, while the resulting bread itself would be light and spongy and would keep well. William Howitt in his letter to Eliza had mentioned the use of carbonate of magnesia in the bread made by the prospectors in Australia. Eliza continued to believe that bakers who mixed magnesia with inferior flour were guilty of fraud, but at least that was better than adding alum or muriatic acid, which she does not mention at all in this book. She did admit, however, that in those years when the wheat harvest was severely hit by bad weather, any wholesome means of rescuing the crop and converting the flour from damaged grain into edible bread was better than leaving thousands of people to starve.

Still in teaching mode, Eliza now progressed to a dissertation on other types of wheat, starting with that from which macaroni was made. She mentioned that macaroni was then being imported into England and that its great value had been recognised as ideal invalid food for those unable to digest bread. During the course of this chapter we are also given a short geography lesson as we learn about the quality of the wheat grown in different parts of the world. 'Supplies from Kent and Essex are reported always as bearing a superior price to all other English wheat; and those from Danzig stand much higher than any other.' We learn that the best wheat was grown in Poland and Pomerania; French wheat was superior to that of England; Italian better than the French – Sicilian the finest in Europe; and the best of all came from the Barbary coast (Morocco, Algeria, Tunisia and Libya) and Egypt. Russian wheat had always been considered to be inferior; but, showing just how up to the minute she was in her research, Eliza reports in another of her footnotes:

> * A new, and exceedingly fine variety of Russian wheat has recently been imported and sold in London at a *very high* price indeed; and I have been informed by the manufacturer, that the excellent preparation called *soujee* is made from a peculiarly hard wheat grown in Russia; it would, therefore, appear that the climate of some parts of that country is not unfavourable to the production of a superior quality of grain.

She had already come across *soujee*; a receipt for Soup of Soujee appeared in *Modern Cookery*, where she explained that it was of Indian origin, similar to semolina. The fine Russian wheat, however, was now being used in the manufacture of *soujee* in England by Messrs Stephens & Co., 2 White's Row, Bishopsgate – another of Eliza's rare endorsements.

The geography lesson was followed by one in history, where we learn that although bread in England, and in most of Scotland, during the mid-nineteenth century was made with wheat, in the time of Henry VIII wheaten bread was confined to the nobility, the poorer classes eating bread made from rye, barley or oats. This persisted until the middle of the eighteenth century in much of the north of England, where little wheat could be grown. Eliza then took her readers through each of the cereals discussing the type of bread which could be made from them. When talking about barley, she mentioned both pot barley and pearl barley, the latter being a greatly refined version of the other and therefore easily digestible and suitable for invalids; pot barley was an important ingredient in broths. Barley water was also much favoured for invalids and is still manufactured mixed with lemon as a refreshing and health-giving drink. One authority quoted by Eliza had expressed regret that unlike some of their foreign counterparts, the English labouring classes did not make more use of the extremely wholesome and nutritious pot and pearl barley. Defending her nation's working people, she says that perhaps it had not occurred to the gentleman concerned that they were deterred from cooking barley, which required a lengthy two to three hours, by the very high cost of fuel. Again, by expressing this opinion, she was hoping to draw to the attention of those in power the fact that high fuel costs affected many other items of food that the poor might otherwise have used.

Having quoted the unnamed authority on oats, too, she moves on to give her own views on maize, or Indian corn, which was at that time a fairly recent import into England. While in no way equal to wheat, she does admit that good bread could be made with it and even went so far as to say that cakes, excellent puddings and savoury dishes could be made without the need to add wheat flour to it. She very much liked the ears of Indian corn boiled and served as a vegetable, which in appearance and flavour she thought resembled fresh peas, telling us that the corn should be scraped from the stems with a knife after it is cooked. No picking up in the fingers for her! And for those readers brought up on Western films and cowboy comics, she even tells us about hominy (grits), a preparation of the whole ripe grain which when stewed or baked for a long period, thus absorbing large quantities of water, produced very cheap and nutritious meals (one pound of grain could produce several pounds of hominy). Giving a scant note on both millet and buckwheat – of no real value in Britain – she gives more time to rice. Again the teacher, she tells us the Hindus live on rice, enlivened by 'the stimulating condiments in which their country abounds', as well as fresh green vegetables and ghee, to the exclusion of animal food. After discussing the various types of rice, she reverts to being the cookery writer and informs her readers that all rice, before it is cooked, should be washed until the water running through it is clear. As if this was not sufficient, she then adds the note: 'If this were generally known by cooks, the wholesome preparation of rice would be much facilitated.' Then she gives us a little insight into her own working methods: 'From a long series of experiments with different varieties of the grain, I have obtained always the same result.'

Part II of the book is subdivided into Section I and II, the first part being titled 'Home-Made Bread'. At last, we are to get the long-awaited bread receipts. But no! This book is to be about every aspect one can think of in connection with bread. In the first few pages, she repeats much of what she has said earlier, even going so far as to quote from *Modern Cookery* about home baking. When talking about the ignorance on the subject, she admits that there are some areas where this does not apply. 'Devonshire is celebrated for the excellence of its household bread (that of the bakers there also is said to be very good); in Suffolk almost every cottager's wife knows how to make it well.' Other parts of England, not specified beyond 'some of our northern counties, and in those where large dairy farms are numerous', are also credited with good bread makers, but 'in Kent, Sussex, Surrey and Middlesex, and many other parts of the kingdom, not one woman in twenty, on the average, is capable of making a loaf!'

At this distance in time it is difficult to understand exactly what Eliza was aiming to achieve with the way this book was turning out. In many ways the structure bears out the contention that she was almost writing a doctorial thesis. For now she gives us a useful table of comparative weight – how much flour would make how much bread – fascinating for the modern reader who has no idea of the old imperial measurements and even more instructive to those brought up with pecks and bushels without ever knowing exactly what they represented. This was followed with a list of all the different ingredients that could be used to make bread or included in its making, such as parsnips and beetroot. A list of different types of flour, the milling process and notes on the storage of flour leads on to a section about varieties of yeast. Again, Eliza shows how much she has read on the subject, quoting at length from *The Chemistry of Common Life* by Professor Johnson.

Section II is entitled 'General Rules for Baking Bread' – but first we need to talk about ovens! We are taken through the various types of oven that were available at the time, ranging from the brick ovens which are still to be found in very old cottages in the countryside to Ball's revolving oven which was an ingenious device suspended from the chimneypiece or, if one had one, from a bottle-jack, in front of the fire. It had the advantage that it could be used in any room provided the bars of the grate were straight and the same width top and bottom. Eliza was very taken with the revolving oven: 'When there is no other oven of any sort in the house adapted to baking bread, this will be found very serviceable, particularly in remote country places and in families who possess but scanty accommodation for domestic purposes.' She then reveals that she had again been actively researching her subject as she tells us: 'There can scarcely be a stronger proof of the value of home-made bread in London than the avidity with which the specimen-loaves are sought which are made by Mrs Ball, and baked in the one or two of her husband's ovens.' This conjures up a lovely picture of Mr Ball demonstrating his oven, perhaps in a large store or in a customised shop, with Mrs Ball proudly producing loaves to be sampled before purchase.

Passing through various instructions and discussions on bread making generally, Eliza finally reaches the point most readers would have been waiting for – the 'Very Plain Directions To A Quite Inexperienced Learner For Making Bread'. Almost immediately, we are back with the Eliza who had spoken to us in *Modern Cookery*, the gentle teacher who is going to be at our side to give us encouragement and spur us on. 'If you have never yet attempted to make bread, and wish to try to do it well, and have nobody to show you the proper manner of setting about it, you may yet succeed perfectly by attending with great exactness to the directions which are given here.' Her instructions are indeed very exact, but once mastered the home baker would be ready to try the receipts that were offered. And these again carry the personal notes with which we have become familiar from the earlier book. We warm to the wife of the Surrey parish clerk, whose bread was in such great demand that she even supplied the family of the clergyman of the parish when his own servants were unable to do so. One is sure that Eliza has met this lady; very probably on the occasions she visited her sister, Susannah, at the home of Robert Webb Smith in Witley in Surrey.

In less than thirty pages, Eliza dealt with the different types of bread one can make, some of them practical, others highly unusual. Then back she goes to the subject of adulterated bread and offers the reader extracts from the report of Dr Septimus Gibbon, the Medical Officer of Health for Holborn. The most interesting point about this report from our point of view is that it was dated 16 March 1857, so we know that Eliza had not completed the book by then. Had Longmans dictated the size of the book, asking for a set number of words or pages? Or was Eliza herself reluctant to let the subject go, realising that this was the last chance she would have to try to form public opinion? There is a certain ragged quality about the last few pages; some are simply paragraphs from pamphlets. Perhaps it was careless editing, but surely, instead of closing the book with a receipt for Bread Chips, To Serve Instead of Biscuits for Dessert, or to Invalids, it would have been more satisfying to finish with Pure Bakers' Bread, where she wrote:

> It is with the greatest satisfaction that I find myself enabled to mention, before I close this work entirely, a movement which has commenced among the better order of bakers for supplying the public with really genuine bread. Some specimens have been sent to me which were truly excellent, and which remained good for so unusual a length of time, that I have no doubt they have been fabricated in a perfectly wholesome manner.
>
> It would, perhaps, be only fair to give the names of those members of the trade who are foremost in the path of improvement; but believing that many others will quickly unite with them in their good and conscientious work, I prefer to wait a little before I add anything to this slight notice of a welcome fact.

So at long last she had the satisfaction, even before her book was published, of knowing that all her campaigning and hard work over the years was beginning to bear fruit. It also shows us that reputable bakers had recognised, as many others did, that Eliza Acton was an authority to be respected. *The English Bread Book* was published on 30 May 1857, priced at 4s 6d.

ELEVEN

LAST DAYS

T he whole of Eliza Acton's life is beset with unanswered questions. If she deliberately set out to deter later attempts to satisfy those curious about anything other than her written work, then she certainly almost succeeded. Even at the end of her life all was not as it seemed on the surface. We know that Eliza was living in London during the 1850s and her death is recorded as having taken place on 13 February 1859 at Snowden Place, John Street, Hampstead. Hampstead would have been the ideal place for her to live, for not only was it considered a healthy location, it was also home to many interesting people. The place abounded with wealthy retired merchants, many from both the East and West Indies; successful London barristers; artists and authors, among them George du Maurier, Ford Madox Brown and Daniel Gabriel Rossetti. And Hampstead had been for many years the home of Thomas Norton Longman, the senior partner in the publishing firm, who, as he returned from his London office one evening in 1841, was unfortunately killed when his horse was involved in an accident. Remembering Eliza's slight dig at the Longmans in her Publisher's Pudding, 'which can scarcely be made *too rich*', she must have enjoyed the irony of ending her own days in such a prestigious area. John Street, where Snowden House was situated, has since been renamed Keats Grove, after the poet who lived there during the years 1818–20. Those who have visited Keats House Museum will appreciate the beautiful Georgian architecture of the pair of semi-detached houses known originally as Wentworth House and Lawn

Cottage, the latter of which Keats shared with his friend Charles Brown. Students of Keats will know, too, that Charles Wentworth Dilke was a great friend of Keats and it was he who had introduced him to Brown, suggesting they might move into the house next door.

One source of information about the past, that bring not only delight to a researcher but also unexpected titbits of interest that may not always be entirely relevant, are the Parish Rate Books, as we found when looking at the Actons' life in Ipswich. Those for John Street, Hampstead, in the 1850s are no exception. The page which contains Snowden House, where Eliza was thought to have lived, is divided into columns that show who lived in each property, who owned it, its designation as a house with the addition of 'with gardens and or stabling', and finally the name of the property. Saint John's Chapel obviously caused the copy clerk some concern as to quite how to describe it and where it should be put, so it straddles the Occupier and Owner columns and the word House is deleted. More fascinating, however, is the entry immediately above it; in the Occupier column there is an indecipherable abbreviation, and after the deleted word 'House' we find 'Vault under the Chapel'.

On a more mundane level, but of interest nonetheless, is the entry for Milford House owned by William Wentworth Dilke, younger brother of Keats' friend Charles and occupied, after 1851 when they moved from Wimbledon, by the family of Philip Hemery le Breton, barrister-at-law. Included in his family was his sister-in-law, Lucy Aikin, well known in her day as a prolific author. Some twenty years older than Eliza Acton, Lucy, who was born in Warrington in Lancashire, the daughter of a doctor, came from a family steeped in literature. Both her father and grandfather were writers, but she was perhaps most influenced by her paternal aunt, the redoubtable Mrs Anna Barbauld.[35] The family were Unitarians, which meant that the men, like all others who dissented from the Church of England, were barred from attending university. Thus education by other means became a focal part of their lives and many excellent Dissenting Academies were set up throughout the country. Although these were not then open to girls, most of the followers of their faith considered it important that women should also receive a good education. Consequently, Lucy was fluent in French, Italian and Latin, and read widely in all of them. As her career developed she translated works into English, made biographical studies of historical figures, and wrote various important treatises, as well as simple teaching aids for use in schools, and captivating stories and verses for children generally. Her output was tremendous. And there she was at Milford House, which, according to the Hampstead Rate Book, was next door to Snowden House. We might assume that the two women, both being writers, had an instant affinity and exchanged visits and had long conversations on literary subjects. It may have been so, but I suggest it certainly would have been so had Miss Aikin been her aunt, Anna Barbauld, instead, for there is no doubt that Eliza was very influenced by that lady when she was growing up. For at that time, Mrs Barbauld was still very well known, not only for her literary work, but also for the major contribution she made in helping her husband make the Academy at Palgrave in Suffolk such a success. Her many talents, including being fluent in Latin, Greek and also modern languages, would have made her the ideal woman for any highly intelligent girl to aspire to emulate. So Eliza and Anna had in common the great desire to educate others, but more important was their shared love of poetry. Was it sheer coincidence or a tribute to a role model, that when Eliza published her poetry she entitled it simply *Poems*, as Anna Barbauld had done in her earliest volume? And was it that controversial essay of Barbauld's showing a sympathetic attitude towards Napoleon that had influenced how the young Eliza regarded him? In the same way that a modern playwright has imagined the spirit of Eliza visiting the young and inexperienced Isabella Beeton to offer her guidance, so it would be interesting to imagine the conversations Eliza might have had with Mrs Barbauld. It is possible that if she did become on visiting terms with her neighbour, the elderly Lucy Aikin, she might have been able to find out more about the woman she had once admired.

Before we have imaginary visits and talk over cups of tea, we need actually to establish Eliza in Snowden House. The Rate Book does not specify who actually owned it; the clerk responsible for compiling the entry may have simply failed to record the ditto marks under John Smith who owned the two properties above Snowden House. It soon becomes clear that many of the houses in John Street (possibly named by the aforementioned John Smith) had been built and sold as rental investments, like much of the rest of Hampstead at that period. For example, all eight properties next to Milford House, described as cottages but were in fact quite substantial houses, were recorded in 1854 as belonging to the executors of C. Pilgrim, whose family had once been major landowners in Hampstead. Snowden House, however, in the May 1854 entry was said to be in the occupation of Mr Robert Muter. So what had he to do with Eliza Acton? And does this mean that Eliza did not move into Snowden House until after 1854? If we are to believe the Rate Books, Muter was still in residence in 1858, so that would mean that Eliza had barely moved into Snowden House before she died.

But Robert Muter was not in Hampstead in 1858; in fact, he must have moved out just after the 1851 census was taken which names only him and his brother William, along with a couple servants, as occupants of the house. Moreover, that same census reveals that living in a house in Bradden, near Douglas on the Isle of Man, were Muter's two children, Caroline and John, with their governess. The census taker noted: 'Head [of house] absent'. Also absent from home was his wife, who was visiting Whitehaven in Cumbria, but without a doubt, by 1851, the Isle of Man was indeed regarded as the family's home and two further children were born there. Robert Muter, who was born in Scotland in 1798, had like many of his fellow Scots gone abroad to seek his fortune, in his case to South America where, with his brother William, he had set up a successful trading company in Rio de Janeiro. Robert came back to England to run the London side of the business and, following his marriage in 1838, moved to Hampstead where his two children were born.

Around 1850 both Robert and William, who had now also returned from Rio in poor health, became members of – that is, investors in – the Royal British Bank. That this had anything to do with his removal to the Isle of Man is open to speculation; neither is it clear if the brothers were in any way implicated in the collapse of the bank that followed in 1856, beyond perhaps losing their investment. Bank failures, usually the result of injudicious speculations on the part of their boards, were not unknown in the latter part of the eighteenth through to the nineteenth century, as readers of *Cranford* will testify; but this one caused not only great losses for its investors, but created a huge national scandal when, in 1857, seven out of the eight directors of the bank were put on trial for conspiracy to defraud the bank's customers.

So it looks as if Robert Muter had sublet Snowden House to Eliza but failed to inform those responsible for updating the Rate Book that he had done so. It is possible that her rent to him covered the rate charges, but it is more likely that under the terms of his lease he was not supposed to sublet, so he simply paid up and said nothing. The question is then posed, did Eliza know the Muters or did an independent agent find Snowden House for her? She may have met the brothers through their banking connection. She might even have invested her money with the Royal British Bank, which might account for her not leaving a will – there may have been nothing to leave.

As an independent single woman it would have been expected of her to make a will, most likely appointing her brother Edward as her executor. However, if she had neglected to do so, then Edward, as her nearest male relation, would have applied for letters of administration on behalf of her estate, but that did not happen either. The fact that by the time of her death Edward himself was ill would not have prevented another member of the family taking the necessary action. So we are left with yet another riddle in the Acton story.

Let us assume we have finally placed Eliza as living in Snowden House during the 1850s. Judging by similar properties in the street, it was a very large house for a lady on her own, so we now have to ask, did she have one of her family to join her? It is very possible that Anna had finally retired from her position as governess to the Corrance family, the youngest daughter having reached an age when she might have gone abroad to a finishing school before being presented at court and 'doing the season', during which time she might find a husband. The two sisters were always very close and it would have made sound common sense for them to make their home together, as later Anna would with Aunt Charlotte and in time Catherine and Susannah. There would, of course, have been a maid or two, as well as a man to look after the garden and generally make himself useful. Anna's role in the household would have been to act as Eliza's companion and housekeeper, for certainly Eliza would not have wanted to worry herself with purely domestic affairs; she had more than enough to keep her occupied. First there was the research for the book on cooking for invalids, which she started in 1851, but then came all the revision of *Modern Cookery* that took her up to 1855. Then she became totally immersed in the research for *The English Bread Book*. This took over the next two years of her life, seemingly leaving her little time to think of other things. One hopes that she did still find time to spend with her friends.

Mary Howitt and her two daughters were now living close by in Highgate. During the period that William and the two sons were in Australia, it is clear that Eliza had regular contact with Mary and the girls. In his letter to Eliza, William Howitt says that she will have had all his news from Mary, which surely suggests frequent exchanges of visits. While in her autobiography, Mary notes an occasion when she had received a visit from M. Reclus, a young Frenchman who was an acquaintance of Miss Acton. This suggests that Mary had met the writer, traveller and later famous geographer at Eliza's home, giving rise to the view that Eliza still entertained an eclectic mix of acquaintances. Always ready to listen to the ideas and work of others, we may wonder how Eliza reacted to the Howitts' growing interest in spiritualism, which had become very popular during the 1850s. It was after Mary and William were commissioned to translate a book on the subject that they became very involved in the practice.

By the time *The English Bread Book* was completed early in 1857 there was strong internal evidence that Eliza had worn herself out. The book had involved her in intensive and difficult research and the labour involved in the actual writing – by hand, of course – and then the final preparations for publication had taken their toll on her both physically and mentally. Again, we are left wondering how Eliza spent what amounted to the last year of her life. Looking back to the doctor's letter to her when she was in Hastings six years earlier, it has been suggested that she might already have been suffering from the early stages of cancer, and certainly she herself stated in the preface to the 1855 edition of *Modern Cookery* that the whole project from its very earliest days had had deleterious effects on her health. For a woman who had been so active both in mind and body it is difficult to imagine her as an invalid, perhaps in terrible pain. If this was indeed the case, it would be reassuring to think that during those last few months she was surrounded by friends and family who brought her comfort and with whom she might still manage to show that sense of humour that had carried her through many difficult times. Above all, it would be nice to imagine her having a peaceful end.

Eliza died on 13 February 1859 at home in Snowden Place. Her death was registered three days later by her sister Anna, who also gave her place of residence as Snowden House. So far, so straightforward. But it is when one looks carefully at the death certificate that questions once more arise. In the column headed Occupation we find not 'Writer' or even 'Poet', but 'Daughter of John Acton of Ipswich, Brewer, Deceased'. This is a timely reminder that although women were by then able to lead independent lives and earn their own living, in the eyes of the law they were still regarded as the appendages and responsibility of men. Had Eliza been married she would have been described as 'wife of – ', and if a widow, the even more archaic description of 'relict of – '. Instead, as a single woman, even one just short of her 60th birthday, she is 'daughter of – '. So that is one question answered, but how to explain what is recorded as the cause of her death, which is given as 'Premature old age. Certified.' A medical expert states that when he was a student fifty years ago, he was instructed that 'Old Age' was not an acceptable cause of death, and a specific complaint or contributory causes had to appear on the certificate. So, if Eliza had cancer, why did this not appear as the cause of her death? Examination of the registration certificates for Hampstead at the time does not reveal that the term 'premature old age' was an accepted term, and the registrar supported my own feeling that perhaps this was a euphemism for dementia.

If this was the case, then perhaps we can understand why the family did not wish to draw attention to Eliza's condition. And so, like Miss Matty in *Cranford*, perhaps Eliza herself, or Anna Potter, thought of 'the desirableness of looking over all the old family letters, and destroying such as ought not to be allowed to fall into the hands of strangers'. It is a tragedy we have come to accept, hard though it is, that minds, even those as sharp as Eliza's, can fail at the end; an end which sadly did not come at the time she had hoped. Thirty-four years earlier she had written:

> ... I would not die
> When Spring hath wak'd the thousand melodies
> Of young birds mounting joyously to heav'n,
> And o'er the earth her emerald vest is thrown,
> Starr'd with bright blossoms, fresh, and beautiful –
> 'Tis sad to be the only withering thing

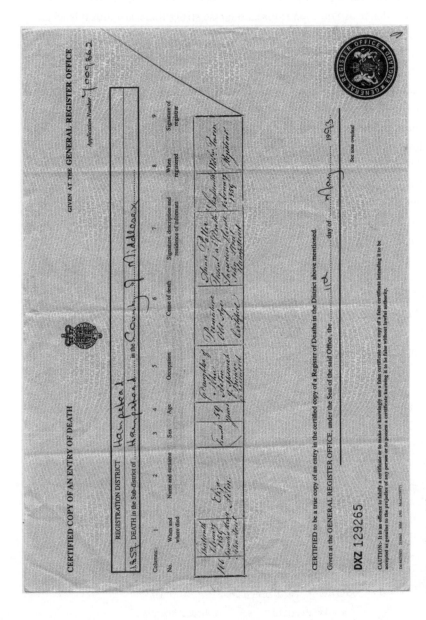

Death certificate of Eliza Acton

Amidst reviving nature! – I would fade

With the last ling'ring flow'rs, whose dirge is sung

By the wild voices of th' autumnal winds!

Eliza was buried by the Reverend W. Wigram in Hampstead parish churchyard on 17 February 1859. There was a 'handsome headstone' (said now to be broken) to mark her grave. The inscription is as plain and direct as she would have wished: 'Sacred to the memory of Eliza Acton formerly of Ipswich who died in Hampstead Febry 13th 1859. E.A. 1859.' Why, after so long away from the town, did whoever chose the wording for the inscription emphasise her connection with Ipswich? Was it that Eliza herself retained much affection for the place and in her last days her memories of early years there had returned to give her comfort? Or was the family conscious that their father always liked to be referred to as 'gentleman' of that place?

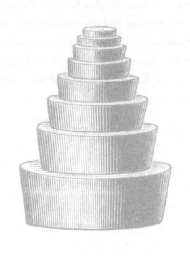

TWELVE

Eliza's Legacy

Eliza Acton died as she had apparently lived, out of the glare of the limelight. She has been described as a shadowy figure so it is not surprising that the only known image of her is a silhouette very similar in style to the more familiar one of Jane Austen. The word 'neat' springs to mind to describe the figure in the reproduction in *First Catch Your Kangaroo*.[36] She appears to be of medium height and slim build; her hair is tied back into the tidy little bun in fashion at the time. Gaze long enough on the profile and one can imagine a little smile playing around her lips. Eliza's silhouette was one of a trio of ladies, all of whom are described on the back as being friends of Anna Howitt, the eldest daughter of Mary and William. Maybe it is a good thing we have no formal portrait of her, it might prove disappointing. Instead, we can make her live in our imagination.

In the same way she left no pictures of herself, neither did she leave any other useful documentation. The lack of a will or even letters of administration for her estate brought to an end the hunt for clues about her life. Her gifts might have thrown a light on, for example, her favourite charities, her religious faith, the affection she held for family and friends, and perhaps an unfamiliar name might have finally proved the existence of the putative daughter. But Miss Acton was not so obliging. This may not have been a deliberate action on her part to deter her future biographers; it is possible that her final illness came too rapidly for her to be able to make the necessary legal arrangements. It is also possible that she had already made gifts of money and possessions to her loved ones. As far as money was concerned, there may have been little to leave, for although her book sales were huge, she had, of course, surrendered the rights of *Modern Cookery* to Longmans four years before her death. The £300 Longman paid for them hardly translates in today's terms into a fortune,[37] but to her it bought security, in the form of an annuity, allowing her to live a comfortable but hardly luxurious life.

But Eliza Acton left a far greater legacy than she could ever have dreamed of. Her *Modern Cookery* was still being bought in large numbers: an advertisement in the *Pall Mall Gazette* in 1873 described it as the 'Six Shilling Standard Cookery Book – 125,000 copies sold'. While in 1884 a new edition appeared with additional plates and woodcuts, priced at 4s 6d, and others followed well into the twentieth century. She had set the standard for good, common-sense cookery in the homes of Britain, the Commonwealth and the Americas. Furthermore, she inspired other cooks to develop her ideas; the setting up of cookery schools produced those well-trained domestics who would go into middle-class homes, while other entrepreneurs made it fashionable for young ladies to be trained in the domestic sciences, learning how things should be done, even if they rarely had to practise them themselves. It was no longer necessary for them to have to go to France or Germany for such training. As the author's mother remarked when her daughter, rebelling against having to help in the house, said she would have servants when she grew up, 'a good mistress needs to know how things should be properly done'. Those female domestic servants trained in the principles of good cookery as laid down by Acton were to become the mothers of lower-middle and working-class families, who knew the value of good, simple and nutritious meals. They were the women who were able to face the shortages of two world wars using knowledge and adaptability to keep their families fed healthily.

Ask again what legacy Eliza Acton left to posterity and the answer that leaps immediately to mind is the one that has caused the most confusion over the years; namely, the very great influence she had on the woman who for generations appeared to supplant her. For most of the young women who grew up in the 1920s and '30s, if they could have only one cookery book, then it had to be Mrs Beeton's. Often awarded as a proficiency prize for girls leaving municipal secondary schools, or given by a grandmother to a bride as a wedding present, Mrs Beeton's *Book of Household Management* became the handbook which would turn a naive young woman into the perfect housekeeper. Yet the book was already very dated, even by then; the lady herself had been dead well over three-quarters of a century, and by the time the 1930s ended, all those chapters on the duties of the domestic staff, menus for dinner parties and how the housewife should organise her day were totally irrelevant. In the 1940s, in some family circles, the book became the centre of a game, 'After the war, I shall eat ...' Players took it in turns to compose a menu chosen from the most outlandish recipes in the book. It also involved poring longingly over the colour illustrations of luscious-looking desserts, such as a Charlotte Russe, and then debating how it was possible to tie so skilfully that beautiful red ribbon round the middle of the pudding?

It has now been fully acknowledged that Isabella Beeton was not the perfect housewife we had been led to believe. In fact, it is doubtful if, beyond the cookery training she received at school in Germany, she ever did a great deal of practical cooking. Others have written at great length about her so this is not the place to add very much, except a personal view that *The Book of Household Management* came to represent the role which women were expected to play in later Victorian England. And when we say women, we need to add the proviso that we are talking of those in that large mass, the middle class, which was rapidly splitting itself into a number of subdivisions. The second half of the nineteenth century saw a great increase in those professions and trades, where either by their education or income some men had been raised in status above those of the working class who laboured to keep body and soul together. This group often included those women who, having worked as servants, had seen at first hand what life was like for those with money and position. Marriage to men who did not require their wives to work meant that the women could aspire to copy the life that had once been beyond them. They too could have servants; they too could entertain; they too could achieve the perfect domestic setting. More and more the idea of woman as the domestic goddess, or 'the Angel of the House', grew, fostered both in literature and art but most of all by the publishers of magazines, of whom Samuel Beeton was hard to match.

Magazines for ladies had long been in fashion, as we know from Eliza's connection with them as a contributor. What was interesting about the new breed of magazines was that they were not limited to 'ladies'; these were intended for that new, wider audience that was to be found in all branches of the middle class. Dickens had recognised the importance of pricing his magazine *Household Words* to within the pocket of the shipping clerk or the student lawyer, and then using it to propagate his own work and that of other serious writers. With his, what we would now call, 'gender neutral' title, Dickens also knew that it was important to include material that would appeal to the family as a whole. Samuel Beeton, a printer/publisher by trade, had quickly realised the potential market to be had among this whole new literate class and rapidly made cheap editions of popular novels, especially ones from America like *Uncle Tom's Cabin*, available to the British public. It was Beeton's *The Englishwoman's Domestic Magazine*, started in 1852, that was to set the pattern for women's magazines for many years to come and would be instrumental in turning his wife into 'a cookery-writer extraordinaire'. There is something solid, dependable and comforting about her very name. Mrs Beeton probably conjured up a picture of a rather large, middle-aged woman who not only knew everything there was to know about cooking in the 1860s, but had also had a vast experience of running her own household. Having 'Mrs Beeton' to hand was like having one's mother or grandmother (or the cook in the large house where one had been a parlour maid) to guide you. Would it have affected sales of the magazine or later *The Book of Household Management* if readers had known that the editress, Mrs Beeton, was in 1857 a young bride of 21? Small wonder, then, that when she first joined her husband on the staff of the magazine to supply the Pickles, Pies and Preserves section, she had to find her copy among the work of others. Like Eliza earlier, she did her homework, reading the books that were already in the market place; but unlike Eliza, she did not test receipts for herself, she simply adopted them as her own. Where a dish was already very well known, then she did acknowledge the creator. She may not have been a cook who had thoroughly learned her craft, but she was more than adept at using words and so happily paraphrased the work of others. Maybe because she was so young, or possibly in order to satisfy the hunger for knowledge that existed in mid-nineteenth-century Britain, she decided also to fill her pages with enlightening topics such as how currants and raisins were grown and prepared. One might argue that in this aspect she was emulating Eliza, the teacher. The difference was that where Eliza 'taught' from personal experience, Mrs Beeton's educational material, like her cookery dishes, was 'lifted' straight from the work of someone else. When Eliza complained bitterly in 1855 that others were plagiarising her work, she could not have known that within a year or so Mrs Beeton would have not only plundered her receipts – a third of Eliza's soups and a quarter of her fish dishes, for example – but would also have taken Eliza's innovation of listing the exact amount required of each ingredient. Clever plagiarist that she was, she put the list first rather than at the end and thus for generations she received the credit for this most important part of every recipe. Beeton has been hailed, too, as the cookery writer who in catering for the middle classes was very conscious of the need for economy. Again, as we have seen, these were ideas she adopted from Eliza. So apart from a propensity to purloin the work of others, why is it that Beeton's work now lacks the freshness of Acton's? The answer lies mainly in the fact that Beeton and most of her predecessors produced household manuals. They gave instructions for the smooth running of every aspect of the domestic sphere of which the production of food was but a part, whereas Eliza wrote exactly what she had been initially asked for – a cookery book. Food may be influenced by fashion and fads, but the basic principles of quality and careful cooking remain the same.

Sales of both their books continued to sell long after they had died, with constant revisions being made with each new edition. Eliza's book was not totally eclipsed by Beeton's; in fact, the two must have existed for many years side by side. It is impossible now to assess how great an impact Eliza's work had on the general public as a whole, but we do know of one individual cook who was influenced by her. It was one of those serendipitous discoveries. While on a tour of the kitchens of Audley End House in Essex, a visitor realised that at home he had the rather battered notebook containing recipes handwritten by his great-great aunt, Avis. She had been employed as a cook in the great house for five years, before she left in 1884 at the age of 46 to get married. Among the recipes in Avis Crocombe's notebook were four copied word for word from Eliza Acton's *Modern Cookery*: Nesselrode Pudding, Gateau de Pommes, a Girlande à la Crème and Charlotte à la Parisienne.

In many ways, Avis Crocombe exemplified the opportunities that Eliza hoped would be available to young working-class women who were properly trained. When we first encounter her in the 1851 census she was aged 13 and working as a kitchen maid at the farm run by her stepbrother in Devon. By the time of the next census she had spread her wings; still a kitchen maid but now part of the staff in a large house in London's Cleveland Square. Of particular historical interest is the fact that the cook in that house was a 34-year-old Frenchman, which shows that the wealthy classes still regarded French chefs as being of superior quality. No doubt Avis was keen to learn all she could from him – and Eliza would certainly have viewed the girl as fortunate to have instruction in the best of French cooking. Ten years later, 1871, we find that Avis has risen to the position of cook-housekeeper in another large household, that of Sir Thomas Proctor Beauchamp at Langley Hall in Norfolk. It would be satisfying to think that, several years later, she was poached by Lord and Lady Braybrooke to cook for them at their Upper Brook Street home in London and, during the shooting season, at Audley End House. This might well be true, but it is more likely that the Braybrookes, who also had been accustomed to employing French chefs, were at that time suffering financially and thus found it much more economical to employ a woman for a much smaller salary. Nonetheless, Avis must have been up to the high standard they expected. From our point of view, it is interesting to know that among the many dishes she had prepared, she felt the need to keep those from Eliza Acton's *Modern Cookery* in her personal notebook.

This pattern of copying recipes from a favourite cookery book is one that has continued down the generations, and often it is finding a housewife's own cook's notebook that will revive a dish from the past. And so we come to what has been, and will continue to be, Eliza Acton's greatest legacy, and that is her influence on successive generations of cookery writers. In finding inspiration for their own work, like Eliza they have studied those of the past, and many have found their way back to Eliza via Mrs Beeton. Once they have found her, they realise her very great contribution to the whole subject of good food, properly cooked and within the means of most. It would be invidious to name names, for in doing so we would risk omitting some whose work, as Eliza would have said, 'is not personally known to us'. Delia Smith has gone on record as stating that in her opinion, Eliza Acton was the most important cookery writer and, in many ways, Eliza's writing mantle has rested for some years upon her shoulders. As far as

Eliza's campaigning zeal is concerned, to improve the nation's eating habits by demonstrating what foods are nutritious and which are positively damaging to health, this has been publicly taken up by Jamie Oliver. He has not always been successful in persuading people to replace junk food with freshly cooked meals, in the same way Eliza battled to get harmful additives taken out of bread. But times are changing. We are beginning to heed her words that 'wilful waste leads to woeful want' as we see how the world's resources are being exploited. And with the current economic pressures, we need to reduce our expenditure on food. More and more people are finding satisfaction in growing their own vegetables and herbs, enjoying not only the better taste but also the money saved. Long-forgotten as well as cheaper cuts of meat are finding their way on to restaurant menus and on to food programmes which show us how best to use them, just as our mothers and grandmothers did in the days of long ago.

Finally, Eliza the teacher and Eliza the campaigner for good nutrition has left to each one of us two important pieces of advice on how to live our lives. The first is 'Eat to live'; the second:

[Be] teachable; be always desirous to learn – never ashamed to ask for information, lest you should appear to be ignorant; for be assured, the most ignorant are too frequently the most self-opinionated and most conceited; while those who are really well informed think humbly of themselves, and regret that they know so little.

APPENDIX I

PRICES IN THE 1850s

Rather than trying to convert the prices charged in Eliza Acton's time into those of the present day, it seems more useful to give some idea of what prices were like in her day. I give them as they were in the pre-decimal coinage of pounds (£) shillings (s) and pence (d). For those who never knew, and those who have forgotten:

A penny was divided into a halfpenny (½d) and a farthing (¼d);

12 pennies made a shilling (s);

20 shillings made a pound (£);

21 shillings made a guinea (gns)

What follows is a random selection of prices taken from advertisements in *The Ipswich Journal*:

Tea – Black:	2s 8d – 4s 0d per lb (depending on quality)
-- Green:	5s 0d
Coffee:	1s 0d – 1s 6d
Cheese – Cheshire:	7½ d per lb
Salted butter:	1/- per pint
Bread:	7½ d – 1s 0d
Eggs:	1s 0d a dozen
Sugar:	3d per lb (variable quality)

Hams & bacon:	8½ d per lb
Cucumber:	4d
Pineapple:	8s 0d
Candles:	7d

Average wage for a labourer: 12s 0d a week

Schoolmaster's salary: £25 0s 0d per annum

Porter & shoemaker at a Suffolk Union House: £20 p.a. + board, lodging & washing

6 Men's Excelsior shirts: 35s 0d

Passage to Australia by White Star Line: from £16 16s 0d

Concert ticket to hear Clara Novello plus orchestra and chorus of 100: 5s 0d, 2s 6d, 1s 6d

Ball tickets – Ladies: 4s 0d, Gentlemen 6s 0d, including refreshments

Rent – 8 bed country house: £80 per annum (landlord paying rates & taxes)

Rent – house and wheelwright's shop, yard etc: £11 p.a.

For sale – house & cottage both let at annual rent of £10 10s 0d

For sale – 3 cottages all let producing £11 0s 0d per annum

Joyce's Patent Laundry Stove – a small efficient stove, useful in summer, heats 6 flat irons, 12 hours for one pennyworth of coke or cinders. A saucepan or kettle may be placed on top. Price 12s 0d

50 guineas – Gentleman's carriage, hardly used, cost 250 gns

Artificial teeth: upper or lower – from £2 0s 0d. Gold – £5 0s 0d

South African Port & Sherry – 20–24 shillings per dozen bottles

Electro-plate: table spoons & forks – 30s 0d per doz.

teaspoons – 10s 0d per doz.

White bone handled knives & forks: 16s 0d per doz

Ivory handled   "   "   £1 5s 0d per doz.

APPENDIX II

THE ACTON FAMILY TREE

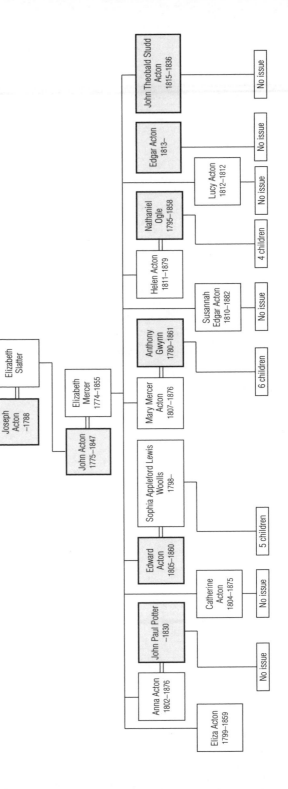

NOTES

1   See John Acton's letter in *The Ipswich Journal* concerning his claim on General Acton's estate.

2   See Sheila Hardy, *Frances, Lady Nelson, the Life and Times of an Admirable Wife* (Spellmount, 2005), Chapter VII, p. 153.

3   *The Pickwick Papers*, Chapter 15. Elizabeth Cobbold was depicted as Mrs Leo Hunter.

4   The Moravian sect grew out of the teachings of Jan Hus, a fourteenth-century Catholic priest who became very critical of the Church. His desire was to return to the 'pure' teachings and practices of the early Church. He was the first 'Protestant reformer' predating Martin Luther. Both the Moravians, who came from Eastern Europe originally, and the Quakers (The Society of Friends) believed that it was wrong to kill and so became conscientious objectors in time of war.

5   This was very popular in Victorian times, both as a painkiller for any number of conditions, as well as a recreational drug. As a painkiller it was a concoction of opium mixed with alcohol, with added sugar to disguise the bitter taste. It was the basis of many patent medicines of the period, hence its frequent use to pacify babies.

6   Lowood School, mentioned in Charlotte Brontë's *Jane Eyre*, is thought to be based on the actual boarding school attended by the Brontë sisters. Dickens also enjoyed describing atrocious educational establishments, particularly Dotheboys Hall in *Nicholas Nickleby*.

7   As nowadays, every house in the parish was valued for taxation
     purposes according to its size and status. Every occupant of a
     property, whether the owner or the tenant, was then required to pay a
     percentage of this value as a Poor Rate. The only exceptions were on
     empty properties or if the occupant was himself described as 'Poor'.
     During the period under review, several tenants in St Peter's were so
     designated.

8   The process of turning barley into malt for making beer was subject
     to fluctuations in taxation – at one point in the 1790s it amounted to
     11½ per cent of the tax revenue. John Acton and his fellow brewers
     were justifiably angry when they found that the tax had been more
     than doubled. Throughout the late eighteenth and early nineteenth
     centuries, many new methods of taxation were found, including
     the introduction of Income Tax; and old ones were increased as the
     government tried to find ways of paying for the wars. Ingenious dodges
     got round some of them, for example the tax on the number of wheels
     on a vehicle resulted in the development of the two-wheeled carriage.
     The infamous window tax led to builders using one very large window
     where previously they would have had two smaller ones, and it was said
     that the fashion for wigs waned with the imposition of the powder tax.

9   See Charles Dickens, *Bleak House*.

10   See Jane Austen, *Pride and Prejudice*.

11   Verses appeared regularly in *The Ipswich Journal*, some of very doubtful
     quality. More entertaining were the verses used to advertise articles
     such as tea or coffee.

12   Fortune telling was a popular pastime of the period and appears in
     various forms in novels such as *Jane Eyre* and *Emma*. Young ladies would
     carefully copy out each card to form a pack ready to be used for an
     evening's entertainment.

13   Robert Barker first exhibited his Panorama in London in 1792. This
     dramatic way of depicting scenes from history, with landscapes painted
     on a cylindrical surface with the addition of scale models, is most
     effective.

14   A chapman: originally an itinerant salesman or pedlar, but here it is used
     as an alternative to the term 'merchant'.

15 Since the Middle Ages, craftsmen had operated a system of apprenticeship. A master craftsman undertook, for a fee, to instruct boys from 14 in all aspects of his trade for seven years. At the end of that time, the young man became known as a journeyman, that is, he hired himself out at a daily rate until such time as he could afford to set himself up as a master of his craft. This system embraced most trades, including that of surgeons, as we see in the case of Edward Acton who was apprenticed to a qualified medical practitioner in Saxmundham.

16 The fourpenny piece or the fourpenny bit was the Victorian version of the silver coin known as a groat. When it was first minted in the 1830s it was also known as the 'fourpenny Joey', after the politician Joseph Hume who was said to have introduced the piece as a convenient payment for a cab fare. It was highly unpopular with hansom cab drivers who, when they had previously been offered a silver sixpence, were told 'to keep the change'. The coin went out of production in 1855 and was only retained for the ceremonial Maundy Money.

17 Marie-Antoine Carême (1784–1833) is regarded as the world's first 'celebrity chef'. Trained as a pastry chef in Paris, he became famous for his elaborate sculptured creations using marzipan, cream, meringues, etc. After working for years for the statesman Talleyrand, he came to England and was chef de cuisine to the Prince Regent, hence his influence on English cooking.

18 See Sheila Hardy, *The Diary of a Suffolk Farmer's Wife, 1854–69* (Macmillan, 1992), pp. 104 & 152.

19 Emma Woodhouse in the Jane Austen novel *Emma*.

20 1845 letter from Fredrika Bremer: see entry in Sources.

21 Upsala: the old established university town in Sweden.

22 Bremer's loved ones were her father and sisters.

23 Translation and notes: courtesy of Rachel Field:

There once was a Lady Delicious –
['tartine' – 1. a fancy open sandwich with a rich or elaborate topping; 2. a slice of bread and jam]
In a beautiful palace of fresh butter.
The walls were made of praline [almonds and chocolate]

The floor was made of crunchy croquets [could be sweet in C18 & C19]
The bedroom of fresh cream,
A biscuit bed,
Curtains of aniseed ...

The story continues (in short):

She married Monsieur Gimblette (a ring-like pastry) etc.
They had a daughter Charlotte with a marzipan nose etc.
Then along comes the wicked witch Carabosse
(a stock figure from traditional tales – a hunchback)
who tips over the sugary palace with her hump.
So, to build it up again,
good parents should give plenty of sugar to their children.

24   Elizabeth Cotton travelling back from France in April 1864 mentions
      in her diary: 'Good passage across the Channel and by express train to
      London. The Custom House Officers very civil and allowed our luggage
      to pass without examination. I said we had Bon Bons etc and they
      replied they would not disappoint my children by stopping their presents.
      Some gentlemen near us were very indignant because the goods they
      were endeavouring to hide were seized.'

25   Muriatic acid mixed with carbonate of soda in the quantities of 4
      drachms of acid to 2 drachms and a scruple to one stone of flour and the
      requisite proportion of liquid was found to produce well-leavened bread.
      When good yeast was unavailable, as it often was, bakers used this as
      an alternative. (See also the chapter on bread and unhealthy additives.)
      Newspapers of the period often advertised the sale of 'genuine new yeast'
      imported from Germany. A drachm was 27½ grains, or 1/16th of an
      ounce, and a scruple was 20 grains. See *The Farmer's Magazine*: Vol. 7,
      1837 – letter to the editor taken from *The Bucks Gazette & Bedford Chronicle*.

26   The extract from William Howitt's letter is taken from the publication *First
      Catch Your Kangaroo*.

27   Sarah J. Hale (1788–1879). A highly educated American woman who
      was a poet, a novelist – she wrote a novel dealing with slavery twenty years

before Harriet Beecher Stowe's *Uncle Tom's Cabin*. She edited a number of magazines, including the prestigious *Godey's Lady's Book*. In asking her to edit the US edition of *Modern Cookery*, the publishers had recognised her as the very best person for the job. She also found time to marry and raise a family. English readers may be surprised to discover that Mrs Hale was part of their early learning: she wrote *Mary had a little lamb*.

28 See Notes on Prices.

29 *Household Words – A Weekly Journal*, 1850–59, conducted by Charles Dickens. Table of Contents, List of Contributors and Their Contributions. Compiled by Anne Lohrli. University of Toronto Press. For anyone interested in nineteenth-century writers this is a fascinating record of stories and articles and how much payment was received for each.

30 Many young doctors were grateful for the opportunity to provide medical care under the Poor Law. This gave them a fixed annual salary in return for which they treated the poor either in their surgery or through home visits, as well as attending to the sick in the workhouse. Further details may be found in Sheila Hardy's *The House on the Hill: the Samford House of Industry* and *Arsenic in the Dumplings: a Casebook of Suffolk Poisonings*.

31 Although the Longman Ledgers mention Miss Acton's *Invalid Cookery* in 1851, I have not been able to trace any reference to the book being advertised. If indeed it was published, there do not appear to be any known copies in existence.

32 At that time butter was still sold by the pint; that is, 16 fl. oz equal to 1lb.

33 See also Cobbett's *Rural Rides* for his 'no hold's barred' overview of the country in the early 1820s.

34 Elizabeth Cotton, in *The Diary of a Suffolk Farmer's Wife*, had for many years an excellent housekeeper who not only looked after the house but acted as a surrogate mother to the children in Elizabeth's absence. However, when she left, Elizabeth decided to employ a cook instead. Unfortunately, none seemed to have absorbed any of Eliza's teaching. Her most frequent complaint was of the cooks being given to a love of alcohol.

35 Anna Barbauld (1743–1825). Another example of a highly educated woman of the period who had a profound influence on the development

of English Romantic Poetry. She was a woman of letters; she learnt Greek and Latin as well as French and German; was an essayist, poet, critic and a children's author. Her life story is fascinating and to be recommended to anyone interested in literature.

36 The silhouette of Eliza Acton appears in *First Catch Your Kangaroo*, which contains the letter to her from William Howitt. A limited edition of 300 copies of the booklet was published and sold by the State Library of South Australia. The ownership of the silhouette has been passed down through the descendants of William Howitt and is presently the property of Mrs Elizabeth Walker. Although repeated efforts were made, the author has been unable to make contact with her.

37 Translating money across the years is in many ways unhelpful, so for that reason I have appended elsewhere a list of prices that were relevant to the 1850s.

SOURCES

Sources consulted or quoted, with permission granted where necessary.

Acton, Eliza, *Modern Cookery for private families* and

———, *The English Bread Book*, Southover Press editions 1993 & 1990
with introductions by Elizabeth Ray

———, *The Poems*, R. Deck, Ipswich, 1826; courtesy of The British
Women Romantic Poets Digital project, General Library, University of
California, Davis

———, 'The Reception', unpublished poem, The British Library Board:
Add.19196, f.189

Aylett & Ordish, *First Catch Your Hare*, Macdonald, 1965

Bradley, Jyll, *Before Beeton: the Story of Eliza Acton*; a play broadcast on
BBC 4 on 21 December 1999. With special thanks to Matilda James
and Jonquil Panting for supplying a recording of the play

Bremer, Fredrika, *The Colonel's Family*, trans. Sarah Death, Norvik Press,
1995

Burman, Carina (ed.), *Fredrika Bremer Brev Ny F ljd (1821–1852)*.
Translations of Fredrika Bremer letters; 21 October 1845 letter – Yale,
Osborn Files, Bremer; 11 May 1852 letter from archives of American
Swedish Historical Museum no 1993-71

Camden History Society, *Buried in Camden*

Fitzgerald, Desmond, *Notes on the Thayer Family taken from Family Notes*,
privately published in 1911, digitalised on the Internet

Hardy, Sheila, *The Diary of a Suffolk Farmer's Wife: 1854–69*, Macmillan, 1992

———, *Frances, Lady Nelson; The Life and Times of an Admirable Wife*, Spellmount, 2005

Howitt, William, *First Catch Your Kangaroo* (which includes a letter to Eliza Acton), The State Library of South Australia, who also supplied a photocopy of an extract from Mary Howitt's *Autobiography*

Lohri, Anne (ed.), *Charles Dickens, Household Words (Accounts Book)*, University of Toronto Press, 1973

Malster, Robert, *A History of Ipswich*, Phillimore, 2000

Pigot's *Directory of Tonbridge, 1840*

Rundell, Mrs, *A New System of Domestic Cookery*, Persephone Books, 2009

Zwanenberg & Cockayne (eds), *Suffolk Medical Biographies*, online

The National Library of Australia, *Sketch of Napoleon's Tomb* in St Helena by C.H. Roberts

The University of Reading: Special Collections – *Longman Archive: A3 Folio 9b p. 9*

Death, Sarah, 'Shaky Puddings: Fredrika Bremer's fictional way with food and drink', originally published in *Gastronomisk kalender, Gastronomoiska akademins årbok*, 2003, pp. 37–57 in Swedish

Gray, Dr Annie, 'Man is a dining animal: the archaeology of the English at Table', unpublished PhD thesis, University of Liverpool, 2009

———, Information on Avis Crocombe and her manuscript cookbook

'History Reheated' (re Avis Crocombe), *The Daily Telegraph* magazine, 24 July 2010

The Ipswich Journal & other newspapers of the period

East Sussex Record Office, Lewes. The Will of Joseph Acton

Suffolk Record Office, Ipswich

FB101/A2/2: St Peter's, Ipswich Overseers & Churchwardens Vestry Meeting

FB101/G9/8&9: St Peter's, Ipswich Rate Books

FB101/G12/1: Rough Sketch of stock in trade of St Peter's, Ipswich

Also consulted:

The Librarian of Tonbridge School

The Archivist, St John's & the Queen's College, Oxford

The Bodleian Library, Oxford University

Census records:

Wills of Robert Trotman; John Potter; Simon Halliday

The Internet was also used to supply other relevant information.

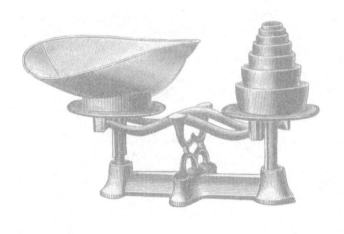

INDEX

Other Biographies by The History Press:

Thomas Hardy: Behind the Mask ....
Andrew Norman

£17.09

Thomas Hardy was shy to a fault and, following the death of his first wife Emma, he burnt a book-length manuscript of hers entitled 'What I think of my husband'. Did Hardy have something to hide, and if so, did it have something to do with Emma? This book pierces the veil of secrecy which Hardy deliberately drew over his life, to find out why his life was so filled with anguish, and how this led to the creation of some of the finest novels and poems in the English language.

978-0-7524-5630-0

Gilbert of Gilbert & Sullivan: his Life & Character ....
Andrew Crowther

£18.00

In his time Gilbert had been many things: journalist, theatre critic, cartoonist, comic poet, stage director, writer of short stories, dramatist. Andrew Crowther examines W.S. Gilbert from all these angles, using a wealth of sources to tell the story of an angry and quarrelsome man, discontented with himself and the age he lived in, raging at life's absurdities and laughing at them.

978-0-7524-5589-1

Jane Austen: an Unrequited Love ....
Andrew Norman

£8.99

Jane Austen is regarded as one of the greatest novelists in the English literary canon, yet much remains unknown about her life, and there is considerable interest in the romantic history of the creator of Elizabeth Bennett and Mr Darcy. Andrew Norman here presents a new account of her life, breaking new ground by suggesting a rift between Jane and her sister over a young clergyman, and proposing an additional reason for her death. A must-read for all lovers of the author and her works.

978-0-7524-5529-7